State Repression and the
Labors of Memory

Contradictions

Edited by Craig Calhoun, Social Science Research Council

State Repression and the Labors of Memory

Elizabeth Jelin

Translated by Judy Rein and
Marcial Godoy-Anativia

Contradictions, Volume 18

 University of Minnesota Press
Minneapolis

This volume was prepared under the auspices of the Regional Advisory Panel on Latin America of the Social Science Research Council, with funds provided by the Ford, Hewlett, and Rockefeller Foundations.

Originally published in Spanish as *Los trabajos de la memoria,* copyright 2002 by Siglo XXI.

Published by the University of Minnesota Press
111 Third Avenue South, Suite 290
Minneapolis, MN 55401-2520
http://www.upress.umn.edu

Library of Congress Cataloging-in-Publication Data

Jelin, Elizabeth, 1941–
    [Trabajos de la memoria. English]
    State repression and the labors of memory / Elizabeth Jelin ; translated by Judy Rein and Marcial Godoy-Anativia.
        p.   cm. — (Contradictions ; 18)
    Includes bibliographical references and index.
    ISBN 0-8166-4283-4 (hard cover : alk. paper) — ISBN 0-8166-4284-2 (pbk : alk. paper)
    1. Political persecution—South America.   2. Victims of state-sponsored terrorism—South America.   3. Memory—Social aspects—South America.   4. Memory—Political aspects—South America.   5. Memory (Philosophy)   I. Rein, Judy.   II. Godoy-Anativia, Marcial.   III. Title.   IV. Contradictions (Minneapolis, Minn.) ; 18.
    JC599.S55 J4513 2003
    323'.044'098—dc21

                                                                    2003013925

Printed in the United States of America on acid-free paper

The University of Minnesota is an equal-opportunity educator and employer.

12 11 10 09 08 07 06 05 04 03   10 9 8 7 6 5 4 3 2 1

This book is dedicated to the memory of my parents, from whom I learned—through their "obstinate memory," with its silences, repetitions, and lapses—the significance of human dignity.

Contents

Preface

The manuscript of this book was in the final stages of revision when worldwide attention was riveted by the attacks on New York and Washington, D.C., on September 11, 2001. The English version of the manuscript was in final revisions at the time of the first anniversary of the attacks, in 2002.

For those who work on memory of repression in the Southern Cone of Latin America, September 11 is a date replete with meanings. Year after year, attention is focused on the variety of expressions that the struggles over memory take up in different segments of Chilean society, as a constant reminder of September 11, 1973, when airplanes bombed the presidential palace, resulting in the death of President Salvador Allende and the installation of a bloody military dictatorship led by Augusto Pinochet. In 2001, the meanings attached to September 11 changed. The coincidence of the dates of these catastrophic and significant events will undoubtedly call for new meanings, and for new material and symbolic referents and anchors for memories of these extreme situations.

Rather than making distinctions between magnitudes of self-inflicted catastrophes, or creating hierarchies of significance or depth of human suffering, I hope that discussions of the issues in this book open the way to a broader reflection on the human need to make sense of catastrophic events and suffering, on memorialization practices, on rituals of homage, and on political initiatives that advance the principle of "never again" in reaction to all affronts on human dignity.

Acknowledgments

This book is part of a dialogue. It does not pretend to offer a full or final interpretation of its subject. Rather, it should be seen as a halt in a longer-term trajectory: assessing developments in the field in order to pose new issues for future work. In this dialogue, which has been ongoing for several years and, I hope, will continue into the future, Susana G. Kaufman occupies a special place. As a continuous interlocutor, her ability to pose questions about her own work and that of others, to learn and to teach, has opened my mind and sensitivity to the multiplicity of dimensions and the complexities of memory, silence, and mourning.

Dialogue has been continuous also with Eric Hershberg, Carlos Iván Degregori, the fellows of the Social Science Research Council's Program on Collective Memory of Repression, and other colleagues and faculty who have participated in that initiative since 1998. I have learned a great deal from all of them, as they have persistently challenged, questioned, and stimulated my thoughts. The consistent support and trust from my colleagues on the SSRC's Regional Advisory Panel on Latin America and the enthusiasm and good disposition of Rebecca Lichtenfeld have been a constant source of encouragement in this endeavor.

Several colleagues and friends read the manuscript and provided detailed comments, generously offering specific insights and suggestions, sharing ideas and concerns: Gerardo Caetano, Ludmila da Silva Catela, Carlos Iván Degregori, Claudia Feld, Alejandro Grimson, Eric Hershberg, Federico Lorenz, Alba Kaplan, Susana Kaufman, Mauricio Taube, and Teresa Valdés. On specific points I also received assistance from Silvina Jensen and José Olavarría. Lucila Schonfeld provided a careful professional edit of the Spanish version, and Mariana McLoughlin assisted with the many details involved in preparing the book.

The English language edition is a slightly revised version of the volume that was published in Spanish in 2002 by Siglo XXI editors in Madrid and Buenos Aires. I am grateful to Marcelo Diaz and his colleagues at Siglo XXI for their encouragement to publish an English translation, and to Craig Calhoun and the staff of the University of Minnesota Press for making that possible. The insightful comments of Andreas Huyssen provided encouragement as well as valuable suggestions about how to make the text more accessible to an English-language audience. The work of translation was undertaken with skill and speed by Marcial Godoy-Anativia and Judy Rein. A careful review of the translation and copyediting was done by Eric Hershberg.

To all of them, and to everyone else who participated in this undertaking—including authors of texts and books with whom my dialogue is imaginary but nonetheless present—I extend my most sincere acknowledgment and gratitude.

Introduction

One cannot want Auschwitz to return for eternity, since in truth it has never ceased to take place; it is always already repeating itself.
Giorgio Agamben, *Remnants of Auschwitz*

Reading the newspapers in Argentina, Uruguay, Chile, Brazil, Paraguay, and Peru at the turn of the millennium may sometimes resemble traveling through a time tunnel. In addition to the obvious economic, political, and police problems of the moment, the news headlines include a number of stories that reflect the persistence of a past that is everlasting and does not wish to pass: the comings and goings of Pinochet's detention in London and Santiago, and his subsequent indictment (and acquittal on the basis of senility and mental health deficiencies) for crimes committed in Chile in 1973; the "truth trials" to clarify the truth about forced disappearances during the second half of the 1970s and the trials to establish the identity of children (now in their early twenties) kidnapped during the military dictatorship in Argentina; the commission investigating the circumstances of the death of former president Goulart (in 1976), and the official procedures to establish who is entitled to economic reparations for victims of the Brazilian dictatorship; the first official recognition that repression and disappearances took place during dictatorship, and the establishment of a Peace Commission in

Uruguay; the coming to light of information contained in documents found in the Archive of Terror in Paraguay; the establishment of a Truth Commission in Peru. This list can be supplemented by the new information about the regional-level workings of Operation Condor being persistently released.

These issues about the past are emerging across the institutional landscape and in the various branches and levels of the state: the executive, the judiciary, national and provincial legislatures, special commissions, the armed forces, the police. The heart of republican institutionality is being pushed to face issues that entail coming to terms with a past that goes back several decades. These news items are returning to the front pages after several years of institutional silence and (apparently unsuccessful) efforts to construct a democratic future without looking at the past. This is so because, as conveyed by the very appropriate title of Patricio Guzmán's film, memory is obstinate, it does not resign itself to remain in the past, insisting on its presence.

In fact, at the level of state institutions, the first half of the 1990s was a low point in actions and initiatives related to human rights violations during dictatorship in South America. It seemed as if a kind of equilibrium between the various political and social forces had been reached. In Argentina, the trials and convictions of the members of the military juntas were followed by legal moves to limit liabilities and by a presidential pardon in 1990. In Uruguay, amnesty laws implemented by the civilian government were followed by an attempt to reverse these laws in a plebiscite, a move that was defeated by popular vote in 1987. In Chile, the installment of the constitutional government in 1990 came hand in hand with a continuing strong position of the military and especially of the commander in chief, General Pinochet. There was only limited debate in Brazil concerning that country's protracted military government. In Paraguay, by contrast, in spite of the continuities in real power and personalized politics, some trials did take place, and soon after the discovery of the *Archivos del terror* opened up the regional dimension of the issues involved. And Peru was at the height of political violence when President Fujimori took office in 1990. Nobody could have predicted that things were going to change so much in a few years.

At the societal and cultural level, however, there were fewer silences. Human rights movements in these countries have maintained a significant presence, linking the demands to settle accounts with the past (demands for justice) with the founding principles of democratic institutions. Those directly affected by repression bear their suffering and pain, which they translate into various types of public action. Artistic expressions in film, narrative, fine arts, theater, dance, and music often incorporate that past and its legacies.

This book seeks to contribute some tools to think about and analyze the presences, silences, and meanings of the past. I will do this on different planes and levels—the political and the cultural ones, the symbolic and the personal, historical understandings and social spheres—building on three central premises or guiding principles. First, memories are to be understood as subjective processes anchored in experiences and in symbolic and material markers. Second, memories are the object of disputes, conflicts, and struggles. This premise involves the need to focus attention on the active and productive role of participants in these struggles. It is they who generate meanings of the past, framed by the power relations in which their actions are embedded in the present. Third, memories must be looked at historically; that is, there is a need to "historicize" memories, which is to say that the meanings attached to the past change over time and are part of larger, complex social and political scenarios. There are also variations in the place assigned to memories in different societies and cultural settings and across the distinct spaces in which political and ideological struggles take place.

The analytic challenges that memory poses cannot be addressed successfully through an itinerary that is linear, coherent, and univocal. Thus, the text explores different perspectives and different approaches to the subject. Some approaches are conceptual and aim to develop analytical frameworks, while others engage more concrete perspectives that cut across studies and reflection about memory. I hope that these multiple approaches converge and shed light on the very elusive subject of the societal construction of memories and meanings of the past. The text may appear decentered. In fact, such is the nature of memory itself. The reader will have to travel through a winding path that touches on the core issues related to memories, with many side trails and detours. Furthermore, the goal is not to offer a definitive text or a definitive clarification of the field; rather, the book is intended to problematize, to raise questions, and to offer reflections that stimulate further studies and dialogues. This approach necessarily means that there will be gaps and undeveloped or underdeveloped themes. To mention just one, the book does not offer an analysis of ethnicity, with respect either to the role of memories in the construction of ethnic communities, or to interethnic or intercultural differences in the conceptualization of time, temporality, and the symbolic location of the past. Nor is there a presentation of the centrality of ethnicity in specific historic processes of violence and repression (such as in Peru or Guatemala). This is a fertile direction of research for colleagues who are better versed in the subject than I am.

Discussion of contemporary memories can rarely be done from outside the scenario where struggles are taking place. The researcher cannot avoid being involved, incorporating his or her subjectivity, experience, beliefs, and emotions, and incorporating as well his or her political and civic commitments. In my case, this includes a strong belief that human conviviality—even among diverse and conflicting groups—is possible and desirable, although difficult. Also, I strongly believe that critical analysis and reflection are tools that, as committed researchers, we can and should offer, especially to the weakest and most excluded members of society, as resources for their process of reflection and empowerment.

The Anchors of "Our" Memories

The urgency to work on understanding memory does not exist outside specific political and cultural contexts. Although this book seeks to present some general reflections, they are offered from a specific vantage point, namely that of unveiling the traces of the dictatorships that governed the countries of the Southern Cone of Latin America in the 1970s and 1980s, and in understanding how these traces unfolded during the post-dictatorial 1990s.[1]

In fact, democratization processes that follow military dictatorships are neither simple nor easy. Once formal democratic mechanisms are instituted, the challenge becomes how best to develop and deepen them. Confrontations inevitably arise over the content of democracy, and this is all the more to be expected in a region such as Latin America, faced as it is with enormous difficulties in virtually all arenas of collective affairs: economic and social rights are increasingly constrained by the prevailing commitment to the market and to neoliberal policies and programs; police violence is ongoing, systematic, and reiterative; the most elementary of civil rights are threatened daily; and minorities face systematic institutional discrimination. All types of obstacles to a true "rule of law" are in evidence. Such realities pose the question as to the continuities and ruptures between the dictatorial regimes and the fragile, incipient, and incomplete constitutional regimes that have followed them. These continuities and ruptures can be analyzed both in terms of everyday lives of different social groups and in terms of the social and political struggles that unfold in the present.

Today, some social and political actors believe that repression and abuses are phenomena of the dictatorial past. Others emphasize the ways that inequality and the mechanisms of domination in the present both reproduce and evoke the past. The recent dictatorial past is, nonetheless, a central part of the present. Social and political conflicts over how to understand and work through the recent repressive past remain active in the present and often are even intensified or deepened. For those who fight for justice for violations of human rights, achievements have been very limited or null. Despite the protests of the victims and their defenders, laws granting amnesty to the perpetrators of human rights violations were enacted throughout the region. For human rights activists, "never again" involves a complete accounting of violations under dictatorship, as well as the corresponding punishment of the perpetrators. Other observers and actors, concerned primarily with the stability of democratic institutions, are less inclined to reopen the painful experiences of authoritarian repression. They emphasize the need to concentrate their efforts in building a better future, rather than continuously revisiting the past. Consequently, they promote policies of oblivion or "reconciliation." Finally, there are those who visit the past to applaud and glorify the "order and progress" brought about, in their view, by the dictatorships. All of these positions reflect ongoing struggles and are tied to current political situations. Some actors may cast them as a continuation of the same political fights they waged in the past, but, in fact, under changed circumstances and faced with new actors, the meaning of the past is inevitably transformed. Even actors keeping the same banners have to assign new meanings to the past that they want to "preserve."[2]

In every case, *once sufficient time has elapsed to make possible the establishment of a minimum degree of distance between past and present,* alternative (even rival) interpretations of that recent past and its memory occupy a central place in cultural and political debates. These interpretations constitute an inescapable subject for public debate in the difficult road toward forging democratic societies. These memories and interpretations are also key elements in the processes of (re)construction of individual and collective identities in societies emerging from periods of violence and trauma.

A basic fact must be established. In any given moment and place, it is impossible to find *one* memory, or a single vision and interpretation of the past shared throughout society. There may be moments or historical periods when a consensus is more pervasive, when a single script of the past is widely accepted, or even hegemonic. Normally, the dominant story will be the one told by the winners of historical conflicts and battles. Yet there will always be other stories, other memories, and alternative interpretations. These endure in spaces of resistance, in the private sphere, in the "catacombs" of history.[3] There is an active political struggle not only over the meaning of what took place in the past but over the meaning of memory itself. The space of memory is thus an arena of political struggle that is frequently conceived in terms of a struggle "against oblivion": *remember so as not to repeat.* These slogans, however, can be tricky. Slogans such as "memory against oblivion" or "against silence" hide an opposition between distinct and rival memories (each one with its own forgetfulness). In truth, what is at stake is an opposition of "memory against memory."

The Itinerary of the Book

This book has a double structure. Each chapter focuses on an issue or question in a sequence that does not follow a single logical or deductive line, although it does follow a script. The script reproduces my own way of questioning and of proceeding in studying the subject, and in that sense there is some order. At the same time, the development of the issues raised takes the form of a spiral, whereby issues raised in previous chapters are revisited in new light later on. These are "turns of the screw" that are meant to allow for deepening the analysis. The intention, I reiterate, is for each reader to be able to use the text in developing his or her own questions, and to advance in the reflective work on his or her own memories and public commitments.

Two additional warnings are in order. First, the book is informed by developments and contributions from a multiplicity of disciplines: sociology, history, anthropology, politics, cultural criticism, psychology, and psychoanalysis. Nevertheless, it is not intended to be a multidisciplinary hybrid. It is focused on social and political actors, their stances in public situations, their confrontations and struggles, and alliances and identifications with others. The analysis deploys concepts and hypotheses offered by several disciplines to enrich understanding of the labors of memory in which social actors are engaged.

Second, although the text is rooted in the experiences of the recent dictatorships in Latin America's Southern Cone, its significance transcends the region. The intent is to contribute to analytical reflection and to the development of issues to be raised for broadly conceived comparative research stretching across boundaries of time and space. The examples, cases, and illustrations presented in the book are drawn from various experiences of extreme situations about which there is substantial research, including the Southern Cone dictatorships but also the Shoah, Japan, and the Spanish Civil War.

The order of the chapters is relatively straightforward. Chapter 1 outlines the current context for paying attention to issues related to memory, and chapter 2 provides a conceptual exploration of the very notion of memory. The construction of memories as products of confrontation and conflict between actors with contrasting narratives is the subject of chapter 3. The focus shifts in the next two chapters, which explore the relationship between history and memory, and the tense role of personal testimonies. Much has been written on these two subjects. Thus, the references to disciplinary academic debates (especially in history, psychoanalysis, and cultural studies) are especially significant for chapters 4 and 5. The last two chapters are more thematic, inquiring into gender and generations, two issues that have received less attention in memory studies. The discussion in these chapters is geared to question and deconstruct "certainties" rather than to provide "truths."

One

Memory in the Contemporary World

We live in an era of collectors. We record and save everything: pictures from childhood and souvenirs from grandmothers in private and family life, newspaper and magazine clippings referring to issues or events of interest, making up official and private archives of all kinds. The past is an object of cult in the West, and this displays itself in the marketing and consumption of various "retro" styles, in the boom of antiques and of historical novels. In the public sphere, archives are growing in numbers, commemorative dates proliferate, and there is a never-ending demand for memorial plaques and monuments.[1] The mass media structure and organize this presence of the past in all areas of contemporary life.

This "explosion" of memory in contemporary Western society has engendered a "culture of memory" (Huyssen 2000) that coexists with and reinforces itself in the context of the high value placed on ephemera, on high speed, and on the fragile and transitory nature of life events. Individuals, family groups, communities, and nations narrate their pasts, for themselves and for others who are willing to visit those pasts, to listen to and look at their icons and remnants, to inquire about and investigate them. This contemporary culture of memory is in part a response or reaction to rapid change and to a life without anchors or roots. In such a cultural climate, memory has a highly significant role as a symbolic mechanism that helps strengthen the sense of belonging to groups and communities. Furthermore, especially for oppressed, silenced, or discriminated groups, the reference to a shared past often facilitates building feelings of self-respect and greater reliance in oneself and in the group.

The cultural debate moves among different interpretations and positions. Those analysts who stress the role of memory as a reaction to the acceleration of contemporary life and as a source of protection against the fear or even the horror of forgetting (as expressed with a touch of nostalgia by Pierre Nora, who laments the disappearance of the "milieux de memoire" and their replacement with the "lieux") seem to place themselves in opposition to those who deplore the pasts that last forever and do not want to move—the apparent "fixations" and returns, the persistence of painful or conflictive pasts, that seem to endure and reappear without allowing one to forget or to broaden the perspective and thus overcome them (Todorov 1998).

Both processes, the fear of oblivion and the presence of the past, take place simultaneously, although they exist in clear tension with each other. In the Western world, this memorialist movement and the concern with memory of painful past events were stimulated by the debates on World War II and the Nazi extermination, which have intensified since the early 1980s.[2] Cultural critics such as Andreas Huyssen theorize about the "totalizing dimension of Holocaust discourse," which "loses its quality as index of a specific historical event and begins to function as a metaphor for other traumatic histories and memories" (Huyssen 2000, 24).

Thus, beyond the cultural climate of the times and the expansion of a "culture of memory" at more general, community, or family levels, memory and forgetting, commemoration and recollections become crucial when linked to traumatic political events or to situations of repression and annihilation, or when profound social catastrophes and collective suffering are involved.[3]

For the individual subject, the imprints of trauma play a central role in determining what the person can or cannot remember, silence, forget, or work through. At the political level, the processes of settling accounts with the past in terms of responsibilities, accountability, and institutional justice are overlayered with ethical imperatives and moral demands. These imperatives, however, may be hard to settle given the political hostilities prevailing in settings where conflict is unfolding and where social catastrophes unleash the destruction of social bonds.

Debates over memories of periods of repression and political violence frequently surface in specific historical contexts and times, namely, when societies undergo political change and there are widespread feelings of urgency to construct democratic regimes in which human rights are guaranteed for the entire population, regardless of class, race, gender, ideological orientation, religion, or ethnicity. The actors participating in these debates link their democratizing projects and their orientations toward the future with the memories of their violent and conflictive past.

Over and over again, actors who struggle to define and name what took place during periods of war, political violence, or state terrorism, as well as those who seek to honor the victims and identify the perpetrators, interpret their actions as necessary steps to make certain that the horrors of the past do not recur—*Nunca Más* ("Never Again"). The Southern Cone of Latin America is an area where this association between past violations and the will of a different future is very strongly established.[4] Likewise, some actors associate the memories of the Shoah and of the Stalinist purges in the Soviet Union with the determination and will to avoid such atrocities in the future. Elsewhere in the world, from Japan and Cambodia to South Africa and Guatemala, the processes of remembrance and the links between a painful past and the expectations for the future may be different, insofar as they are set in different cultural frames and thus may have alternative ethical and political meanings.

The Complexities of Time

The framework presented above locates the meanings of the past unequivocally in the present and in relation to a desired future. If we add the existence of multiple subjectivities and time horizons, it is clear that we are facing an inherently or essentially complex issue. What then are the temporal dimensions at stake here?

A first way to conceptualize time is in a linear or chronological manner. Past, present, and future are ordered in a clear way—one could even say "naturally"—in a physical or astronomical time frame. The units of time are equivalent and divisible: a century, a decade, a year, or a minute. However, as soon as historical processes and human subjectivities are introduced into the picture, the complexities involved come to light. As expressed by Reinhart Koselleck (1985), "historical time, if the concept has a specific meaning, is bound up with social and political actions, with concretely acting and suffering human beings and their institutions and organizations" (xxii). And when studying these concrete human beings, the sense of time and temporality are established in a different way: the present contains and constructs past experience and future expectations. "Experience is present past, whose events have been incorporated and can be remembered" (272).

Experiences are also shaped by the "horizon of expectations," thus introducing a reference to a future temporality. Expectation is "the future made present, it points to the not-yet, to that which has not been experienced, to that which can only be discovered" (Koselleck 1985, 272). It is at that point of complex intersection and convergence, in that present where the past is the space of experience and the future is the horizon of expectations, where human action is produced.

Locating memory in time implies making reference to the "space of experience" in the present. Remembrances of the past are incorporated there, although in a dynamic manner, since experiences incorporated in a given moment can be modified in subsequent periods. "The events of 1933 have occurred once and for all, but the experiences which are based upon them can change over time. Experiences overlap and mutually impregnate one another" (Koselleck 1985, 274–75).

There is an additional element in this complexity. Human understanding embodies personally lived experiences; it also incorporates secondhand experiences—those that are conveyed by others. The past, therefore, can be condensed or expanded, according to how these diverse past experiences are integrated.

In sum, we are referring to subjective processes of assigning and changing meaning, whereby the actors move and orient themselves (or disorient and lose themselves) among "past futures" (Koselleck 1985), "lost futures" (Huyssen 2000), and "everlasting pasts" (Conan and Rousso 1994). All this takes place in the present, which must simultaneously come close to and distance itself both from the pasts accumulated in the spaces of experience and from the futures included as horizons of expectations. Furthermore, these temporal meanings are constructed and change in relationship to and in dialogue with others who, individually and collectively, can share and/or confront the experiences and expectations. In turn, new historical processes, as well as changing social and political conjunctures and scenarios, inevitably produce alterations in the interpretive frameworks for understanding past experience and for constructing future expectations. The complexity, then, refers to the multiplicity of temporalities at play, the multiplicity of meanings, and the ongoing transformation and change in actors and historical processes.

The Labors of Memory

The title of this book alludes to memory as labor. Why refer to the *labors* of memory? As a distinctive feature of the human condition, work is what puts the individual and society in an active and productive position. The person is an agent of transformation, and in the process transforms him or herself and the world. Activity adds value. Thus, to assert that memory involves "labor" is to incorporate it into the activity that generates and transforms the social world.

To talk about the *labors* of memory demands establishing some important analytical distinctions. Undoubtedly, some events lived in the past have effects on subsequent periods, independently of the will, consciousness, agency, or strategy of the actors involved. Such effects show up in "objective" social and collective facts, such as losing a war and therefore being under the domination of foreign powers. They also are inherent in more personal and unconscious processes associated with traumas and voids. The presence of the past can disrupt, penetrate, or invade the present as something that makes no sense, as mnemonic traces (Ricoeur 2000), as silences, compulsions, or repetitions. In such situations, the memory of the past intrudes, but it is not the object of labor. It is a presence without agency. The flipside of these involuntary intrusions takes place when human beings are actively involved in the processes of symbolic transformation and elaboration of meanings of the past. Human beings who "labor" on and with memories of the past.

The events of the past, and the attachment of the person to that past, especially in cases of trauma, can involve a fixation or a constant return: the compulsion to repeat or to act out, the inability to detach oneself from the lost object. Repetition involves, in this case, acting out again and again the same pattern. There is no sense of distance from the past, which reappears and makes its way, like an intruder, into the present. Even observers and secondary witnesses can become participants in acting out or repetition, through processes of identification with the victims. There is a dual danger in such situations: the menace of an "excessive" presence of the past in ritualized repetition and in the compulsion to act out, and the menace of a selective forgetting, a void that can be subject to manipulation by the self or by others.

To overcome such situations requires considerable labor, working through the painful memories and recollections instead of reliving them and acting them out. Psychoanalytic theory refers to this as the labors of mourning. Mourning involves an "intrapsychic process, following the loss of an object of fixation, through which the subject achieves progressive detachment from the object" (Laplanche and Pontalis 1981, 435). In this process, the psychic energy of the person is released from being "occupied by pain and recollections," and the subject is able to recover his or her freedom. This labor requires time, "it is carried out piece by piece, with an expenditure of time and energy . . ." (Freud 1976, 243). It involves being able to let go and forget, and to transform attachments and feelings, breaking the fixation on the other and on the pain, accepting "the satisfaction brought about by the very fact of being alive" (243).[5] It involves a period of mourning, and "the labor of mourning reveals itself, not without difficulties, as a liberating exercise to the extent that it consists of memory work" (Ricoeur 1999, 36).

Acting out and repetition can be contrasted to the idea of working through. The Freudian notion of working through, conceived in a therapeutic context, consists of the "process through which the patient under analysis accepts and incorporates an interpretation, overcoming the resistances that it evokes. . . . [It is a] type of psychic labor that allows the subject to accept certain repressed elements inside himself, thus liberating himself from the spell of repetitive mechanisms" (Laplanche and Pontalis 1981, 436). Working through is no doubt a form of repetition, yet modified by interpretation. Thus, it predisposes or encourages the subject to work on his or her repetitive mechanisms (437).

These notions of working through and acting out can be applied and extended outside the therapeutic context. In working through, according to LaCapra (2001), "the person tries to gain critical distance on a problem and to distinguish between past, present and future. . . . There may be other possibilities, but it is via the working through that one acquires the possibility of being an ethical and political agent" (143–44).

At the level of the individual, acting out and working through turn out to be coexisting forces. Involved with the tension among these two forces, the person has to face the threat that the process of working through may awaken a sense of betrayal and a feeling of weakening the loyalty to the lost object. Taken to the ethical and political level, this tension implies the active incidence of social forces that push for maintaining and reinforcing the repetitive acting out of the past. It is as if repetition (even compulsive repetition) would make possible avoiding the closure and forgetting presumably implied in the process of working through. To quote LaCapra (2001):

> The result is a paralyzing kind of all-or-nothing logic in which one is in a double bind: either totalization and the closure you resist, or acting out the repetition compulsion, with almost no other possibilities. Within this constricted frame of reference, politics often becomes a question of blank hope in the future, an openness toward a vacuous utopia about which you can say nothing. And this view very often links up with an apocalyptic politics or perhaps a politics of utopian hope in the form of indefinite deferral of institutional change. . . . (145)

At the collective level, the big challenge is to overcome repetitions, to surmount silences and political abuses, to simultaneously be able to distance from and promote an active debate and reflexivity about the past and its meaning for the present/future. Concerned with the "abuses of memory" (stemming from moral mandates to remember, which generally involve repetitions rather than a process of working through), Todorov (1998) seeks a way out by trying to abandon the emphasis on the past in order to place it on the future. This involves a difficult journey for subjective processes: distancing oneself from the past, and "learning to remember." For the public and political sphere, it involves rethinking the relationship between memory and politics and between memory and justice.

Two

What Memories Are We Talking About?

The draft title for this chapter was "What is memory?" Such a title invites a single and univocal definition of the term. Though not involving a logical contradiction, asking what memory *is* (in singular) may seem at odds with offering to study processes of memory construction, of memories in the plural, and of social disputes over memories, their social legitimacy, and claims to "truth." This chapter attempts to advance some conceptual issues in order to offer some tools for further analytical and empirical steps. It does not pretend to be an exhaustive discussion of issues that, by their very complexity, are inherently multi-dimensional and open-ended. Dealing with memories entails paying attention to remembrance and forgetting, to narratives and acts, to silences and gestures. Knowledge and information are at play, but so too are emotions, lapses, voids, and fractures.

A first issue to consider is the subject who remembers and forgets. Is the subject always an individual, or is it possible to talk about collective memories? The social sciences have devoted countless pages to answering this question, which is yet another manifestation of the eternal tension and dilemma of the relationship between individual and society.

A second issue refers to the content of what is remembered and of what is forgotten. No doubt, the core of what is remembered and forgotten relates to direct personal life experiences. Yet even the most intimate incidents are always mediated by mechanisms of social interaction, involving links between the manifest and the latent or invisible, the conscious and the unconscious. Memory also incorporates knowledge, beliefs, behavior patterns, feelings, and emotions conveyed and received in social interaction, in processes of socialization, and in the cultural practices of a group.

Additionally, there is the issue of how and when remembrance and forgetting occur. The past that is remembered and forgotten is activated in a present and in relation to future expectations. Be it within the dynamics of the individual, in interpersonal social interactions, or in more general or macrosocial processes, certain memories are activated in special moments or conjunctures; in other moments, silences and even forgetting prevail. There are also other ciphers for the activation of memories, expressive or performative in nature, in which rituals and myth occupy privileged places.

Intellectual and Disciplinary Traditions

Memory as "the mental capacity or faculty of retaining and reviving facts, events, impressions, etc., or of recalling or recognizing previous experiences" (*Random House Webster's Dictionary* 1998, 1199) has always intrigued humanity. Indeed, what most concerns people is *not* remembering, not being able to retain events of the past in memory. At the individual level and in daily interaction, our lives go on accompanied by the unremitting and perpetual enigma of not understanding why we do not remember a familiar name or a date, why we store and have available so many and varied "useless" recollections, and why surprising associations and memories crop up at unexpected times or places. And the fear of memory loss when aging haunts us permanently.

At the group or community level, or even socially or nationally, the enigmas are just as compelling. The question of how remembering or forgetting occurs arises from the anxiety and even the anguish generated by the possibility of forgetting. The fear of oblivion and forgetting, or that of being forgotten by others in the future, has come to be interpreted in the contemporary Western world in terms of the threat to personal and cultural identity.

In the first place, the issue revolves around the psychological ability to remember and forget, in mental processes that are the domain of psychology and psychiatry. Developments in neurobiology locating memory centers in the brain and studying the chemical processes involved in memory are complemented by significant research on the "paths" and circuits of memory and memory loss and errors (Schacter 1996, 2001).

In a different direction, psychoanalysis is concerned with another quality of the mystery, paying attention to the role of the unconscious in the search for an explanation of the blocks, lapses, voids, and repetitions that the conscious ego cannot control. The influence of psychological processes involved in the development of the ego and the notion of trauma (a topic we will return to later) are central to this field. This line of inquiry goes beyond examining memory and forgetting from a cognitive perspective interested in how much and what is remembered or forgotten. It introduces unconscious emotional and affective factors when considering "how" and "when" memory works.

The exercise of the abilities for remembering and forgetting is unique. Each individual has his or her "own memories," and they cannot be transferred to others. It is this singularity of memories and the possibility of activating the past in the present—memory as the present of the past, in the words of Paul Ricoeur (1999, 16)—that defines personal identity and the continuity of the self over time.

These processes, we know, do not take place in isolated individuals, but in human beings embedded in networks of social relations, groups, institutions, and cultures. At this juncture, the passage from the individual to the social and interactive level is unavoidable; the move follows its own seamless course. It is human beings who have the capacity to remember, and they are always located in specific group or social contexts. It is impossible to remember or re-create the past without alluding to those contexts. The question debated at length in the literature is the relative weight of the social context and the individual in the memory process. Thus, to borrow the apt expression from a recent study, the question is how to combine *homo psychologicus* and *homo sociologicus* (Winter and Sivan 1999).

Two stylized models for thinking about the social dimension in memory processes can be advanced. These models reproduce the debates within the classical traditions of sociology. Maurice Halbwachs is the central figure in these debates, anchored in his writings about the social frameworks *(cadres)* of memory (published in 1925) and about collective memory (published posthumously) (Halbwachs 1994, 1997). His ideas have generated numerous readings and interpretations, including annotated critical analyses (Coser 1992; Namer 1994; Olick 1998a; Ricoeur 2000). There are several points for debate and controversial understandings: whether Halbwachs allows space for individualities in the field of collective memory; if it is possible to have such a thing as a "collective memory"; or whether these are purely collective myths and beliefs, where memory does not have a place (Hynes 1999).

It is not my intention to enter into that debate or provide a new interpretation of Halbwachs's ideas here. There is a key insight in his work, and this is what should be stressed, namely the concept of social *cadres* or frameworks. Individual memories are always socially framed. These frameworks bear the general representations of society, its needs and values. They also include the worldview and language of a society or group. For Halbwachs (1992), this means that "we can remember only on condition of retrieving the position of past events that interest us from the frameworks of collective memory. . . . Forgetting is explained by the disappearance of these frameworks, or of part of them" (172). This entails that the social is always present, even in the most "individual" moments. "We are never alone"—one does not remember alone but with the help of the memories of others and of shared cultural codes, even when personal memories are unique and distinct. These personal recollections are immersed in collective narratives, which are frequently reinforced in group rituals and commemorations (Ricoeur 1999). Insofar as the frameworks of memory are historical and subject to change, all memories are more reconstructions than recollections. Anything that does not find a place or a meaning in that framework is material that can be lost and forgotten (Namer 1994).

Can the existence of collective memory be asserted? And if so, what is collective memory? Some readers of Halbwachs interpret his emphasis on a collective memory as an affirmation of its "real" existence as a "thing" independent of individuals. However, if emphasis is placed on the notion of "social framework"—a view that, in my understanding, is more productive for our objectives—the interpretation shifts toward a focus on the group matrix within which individual recollections and silences are set. These frameworks—Halbwachs looks at the family, religion, and social class—provide meaning to individual recollections.[1]

In fact, the very notion of "collective memory" presents serious difficulties if it is understood as a reified entity, a thing that has an existence that is separate and above that of individuals. Such a conception originates from an extreme Durkheimian interpretation that takes social phenomena as "things." Alternatively, the "collective" can also be construed in the sense of shared memories, layered on each other—as the outcome of multiple interactions structured by social frameworks and power relations. In this vein, the collective aspect of memory is the interweaving of traditions and individual memories in dialogue with others and in a state of constant flux. The outcome is not a chaotic disorder, because there is some structure shaped by shared cultural codes and some social organization—where some voices are stronger than others because they have greater access to resources and to public stages. As Ricoeur (1999) says,

> collective memory simply consists of the set of traces left by events that have shaped the course of history of those social groups that, in later times, have the capacity to stage these shared recollections through holidays, rituals, and public celebrations. (19)

This perspective allows one to conceive of collective memories not only as facts that are out there, "given" and preexistent. It calls for placing primary attention on the processes of development and social construction of these memories. This implies incorporating the agency of different social actors (including marginalized and excluded groups), and the disputes and negotiations over meanings of the past in different settings (Pollak 1989). It also leads to leaving open to empirical research the question as to the conditions that foster the existence (or lack) of dominant, hegemonic, unique, or "official" memories.

A further significant distinction in memory processes is between active and passive memories. Remains and vestiges of the past, even recognizable knowledge and information, can be kept passively archived in people's minds, in registers, in public and private archives, in electronic formats, and in libraries. The accumulation of such traces of the past have led some analysts (Nora especially) to talk about a "surplus of memory." However, these are passive reservoirs that have to be set apart from their use, the labor and human activity connected with memory work. At the individual level, cognitive psychologists distinguish between *recognition* (a cognitive association or connection, the identification of an item with reference to the past) and *recall* (which implies a personal evaluation of what is recognized, entailing a more active effort on the part of the subject). The mnemonic traces of recognition seem to last longer than those of recall. At the societal level, there may be an abundance of archives and documentation centers, even of accumulated knowledge and information about the past, with traces in various types of recognized vehicles and material supports. Yet all these supports and props do not guarantee that the past will be recalled, or the specific meanings that groups will attach to its traces. To the extent that recall is activated by social subjects and is mobilized in actions intended to give meaning to the past, by interpreting it and bringing it onto the stage of the current drama, the process of recalling becomes central in the process of social interaction.

A note of caution is required here to avoid the pitfalls of extreme ethnocentrism or essentialism. It should be clear by now that memories are constructed and acquire meanings within specific social frameworks embedded with values and social needs shaped by particular worldviews. This conception could imply, in a first naive understanding, that the content of memories being constructed is contained and shaped by a clearly set and unchanging conception of past, present, and future. In such a view, there is no room for diversity in the conception of time itself. Notions of time would thus appear to stay outside the social frameworks and the actual processes of "framing" memories. A second reading is therefore needed, one that avoids essentializing time conceptions and taking the Western conception of time as universal. As Halbwachs indicated, the concepts of time and space are themselves objects of construction and social representation. Although all processes of memory construction are inscribed in a given representation of time and space, these representations—and consequently, the very idea of what is past and what is present—are culturally variable and historically constructed. Of course, this includes the analytical categories used by researchers and scholars.

At this point, anthropological and historical research has to come into the picture, to enrich the analysis with the diversity of ways of conceiving time and, consequently, of conceptualizing memory. Classical anthropology did, in fact, develop itself in contradistinction to history. It was the study of "peoples without history." And if there is no history, then there cannot be historical memory, since the present is seen as an unending repetition and reproduction of the past. In many past and present societies, that which is experienced as "real" is not historical temporality but a mythical time that returns permanently, in rituals and repetitions, to an original foundational moment. However, the ritualized performance of myth is not static. In such cases, the issue is not about ahistorical societies. Rather, the issue becomes to show how the "new" events are incorporated into preexisting structures of meaning, which at times can be anchored in myths. Thus, "every reproduction of culture is an alteration" (Sahlins 1987, 144), and the re-presentation of myth implies change.[2] In such cases, what is "remembered" is the cultural framework of interpretation, a tool that facilitates the understanding of circumstances that viewed from the outside seem "new," although they may not be seen as such by the actors involved.

Alternatively, there are traditions and customs incorporated as nonreflective daily practices that have lost their original meaning in the evolution and historical changes of the times. The Inquisition, for example, forced many Jews to convert to Catholicism, and many maintained private clandestine traditional Jewish practices (the so-called *Marranos*). After several generations, some practices may have been maintained, although devoid of their original meanings. Examples include deep housecleaning on Fridays in a rural Brazilian village, and Stars of David on Catholic tombs in some Portuguese towns.

Memory and Identity

There is a sphere in which the relationship between memory and identity is almost banal, but nevertheless important as a point of departure for reflection: the heart of any individual or group identity is linked to a sense of permanence (of being oneself, of selfhood) through time and space. The ability to recall or remember something from one's own past is what sustains identity (Gillis 1994). The relationship is one of mutual constitution in subjectivity, since neither memories nor identity are "things" or material objects that are found or lost. "Identities and memories are not things we think *about,* but things we think *with.* As such, they have no existence beyond our politics, our social relations, and our histories" (5).

This relationship of mutual constitution entails a give and take: to establish some parameters of identity (national, gender, political, or any other type), the subject selectively takes certain signposts, certain memories that place him or her in relation to "others." The boundaries of identity are established by these parameters, which simultaneously stress some features of identification (and belonging) with some groups and of differentiation with others. In this process, they become social frames that structure memories. Some of these signposts develop into "unvarying" or fixed elements around which memories are organized. Pollak (1992) refers to three types of elements that can fulfill this signpost function: events, persons or characters, and places. They may be linked to experiences lived by the person or conveyed by others. They can be empirically based on concrete facts or be projections or idealizations stemming from other events. What matters is that they allow the maintenance of the minimum of coherence and continuity needed to preserve the sense of identity.[3]

The constitution, institutionalization, recognition, and strength of memories and identities fuel each other. Both for individuals and for groups or entire societies, the processes are not linear over time. There are periods of tranquility and calmness, when life goes on without disturbances, and times of crises. During periods when memories and identities are firmly constituted, strongly attached, or even institutionally established, the challenges that might emerge do not generate urgencies, they do not lead to major restructuring processes. Memory and identity can work by themselves and on themselves in an effort to maintain coherence and unity. Periods of internal crises or external threats are usually preceded, accompanied, or succeeded by crises in the sense of collective identity and in memories (Pollak 1992). In such moments, the unsettling of taken-for-granted interpretations of the past leads to self-reflexivity and revisions of the prevalent meaning attached to the past. At the same time and in the same movement, they involve questioning and redefining group identity itself.

Memories and Forgetting

Everyday life is primarily made up of routines: patterns of behavior that are habitual, nonreflective, learned, and repeated. The past of the learning process and the present of its memory turn into habit and tradition (understood as "the handing down of statements, beliefs, legends, customs, information, etc., from generation to generation, especially by word of mouth or by practice" [*Random House Webster's Dictionary* 1998, 2006]). Habitual and traditional beliefs and practices are part of "normal" life. There is nothing "memorable" in the daily exercise of these memories. Exceptions—not very frequent in any case—occur when the person associates some routine practice with the recollection of some incident of failure of the learned routine, or with some childhood episode in the process of personal learning.

These patterns of behavior, clearly "framed" (in Halbwachs's sense)

socially in the family, the classroom, and the traditions of other institutions, are both individual and social. They are incorporated in
a unique way by each person. At the same time, they are shared and
recurring in all members of a social group. Clothing and table habits,
manners of greeting men and women, strangers, and close friends,
body language employed in public and in private, forms of expressing
feelings—all these are simple examples of shared learned practices.
The list of learned patterns of behavior where a "habitual memory"
functions in a routine manner is interminable.

Fractures in these learned routines involve the subject in a different
way. Emotions and feelings come into play, occupying center stage.
As Mieke Bal (1999, viii) argues, it is that emotional commitment
that transforms these moments and turns them "memorable." This
memory is a different one, transforming itself. The event or moment
being remembered is then associated with emotions and feelings, and
this association sets in motion a process of search for meaning. In turn,
the "memorable" event will be expressed in narrative form, becoming
the *way in which the subject bestows meaning to the past*. In this way,
memory expresses itself in a narrative story, which can be conveyed
to others.

This narrative construction has two central features. First, the
past acquires meaning in its intersection with the present, in the act
of remembering/forgetting. Second, the interrogation of the past is
a subjective process. It is always active and socially constructed in
dialogue and interaction with others. The act of remembering implies
having lived through a given event in the past that is activated in the
present, as a result of some current desire or distress. Often, this active recollection is accompanied by the intent of communicating it
to others. It does not necessarily entail that the events being recalled
were important or significant in themselves, but rather that they gain
an emotional charge and a special meaning in the actual process of
remembering or recalling.

This narrative memory entails, in the words of Micheline Enriquez,
constructing a "new arrangement" between the past and the present.[4]
A number of social and psychic mechanisms come into play. The process of constructing and conveying narrative memories involves complex negotiations about what is acceptable and what is to be silenced,
what can and cannot be said, in the disjunctions between private narratives and public discourses. Socially accepted narratives, publicly

accepted commemorations, social frameworks, and societal mechanisms of censorship—along with the more personal and intrapsychical drives—leave their imprints in such negotiations, as shown in the large body of research on Eastern Europe and the testimonies of concentration camp survivors (Passerini 1992b; also Pollak 1989, 1990).

In turn, although they may reappear in different ways in future instances, some past events resist the possibility of being integrated in a narrative and remain without a clear meaning. Traumatic events involve breaks in the ability to narrate and memory voids and gaps. As will be further developed later, the presence of trauma is indicated by the coexistence of an impossibility of assigning meaning to past occurrences, by the inability to incorporate it in a narrative, and by its recurrent and persistent presence and manifestation in symptoms. At this level, oblivion is not an expression of absence or emptiness. Rather, it is the presence of that absence, the representation of something that is no longer there, that has been erased, silenced, or denied. Like Milan Kundera's photo, it is a manifestation of a social vacuum.[5] The clinical equivalent of these traumatic gaps takes the form of voids, symptoms, and repetitions.

Up to this point we have distinguished two types of memories, habitual and narrative. The narrative memories are the ones that are of interest here. Among them, there are those memories that find or construct meanings of the past. And there are—a situation especially important to our analysis—the "wounds of memory," an expression that is more precise than "wounded memories" (the latter expression is used by Ricoeur 1999). These wounds imply great difficulties for constituting meaning and building its narrative. They refer to situations where repression and dissociation act as the psychic mechanisms that lead to interruptions, breaks, and traumatic gaps in narrative. Traumatic repetitions and dramatizations are "tragically solitary," while narrative memories are social constructions communicable to others (Bal 1999).

Forgetting and silence play a central role in narrative memory. All narratives of the past involve silences. Memory is selective; full memory is impossible. Thus, there is a first type of forgetting, "necessary" to the functioning of the individual subject, of groups, and of communities. But there is more to silence and forgetting, since there is a multiplicity of situations in which many different forms of forgetting and silences are expressed, with different purposes.

One type of forgetting, which can be called deep or "definitive," involves the erasure of recollections of facts and processes of the past and is produced within historical development itself.[6] The paradox is that if total erasure is successful, its very success impedes its verification. Nevertheless, there are cases when pasts that seemed "definitively" forgotten reappear as a result of changes in cultural and social frameworks and acquire a new symbolic or political presence. Those changes prompt a reexamination and the assignment of new meanings to traces and residues that had not been significant for decades or even centuries.

Erasures and voids can also be the results of explicit policies furthering forgetting and silence, promoted by actors who seek to hide and destroy evidence and traces of the past in order to impede their retrieval in the future. Recall Heinrich Himmler's famous statement at Nuremberg, declaring that the "final solution" was a "glorious page in our history that has never been written and that never will be."[7] In these cases, there is a willful political act of destruction of evidence and traces, with the goal of promoting selective memory loss through the elimination of documentary evidence. In a broader sense, all policies for conservation and memory, by selecting which artifacts and traces to preserve, conserve, or commemorate, have an implicit will to forget. This is true of course for the historians and researchers who choose what to tell, what to represent, what to write, and how to do it.

The past leaves *traces,* in material ruins and evidence, in mnemonic traces in the human neurological system, in individual psychical dynamics, and in the symbolic world. In themselves, these traces do not constitute "memory" unless they are evoked and placed in a context that gives them meaning. A further question thus arises: how to overcome the difficulties involved in accessing these traces, to preclude oblivion. The task involved implies uncovering and revealing, bringing to light the hidden, "crossing the wall that separates us from these traces" (Ricoeur 1999, 105). The difficulty is not that few traces remain, or that the past has been destroyed. Rather, what count are the impediments to accessing those traces caused by the mechanisms of repression and by displacement,[8] which cause distortions and transformations in different directions and of diverse types. Psychoanalysis has worked extensively on the issue of the recovery of personal memories. As well, recent developments in historiography and social sciences attempt to deal with the social and collective processes of unearthing hidden pasts.

One societal response to the fear of destruction of traces of the past is reflected in the contemporary expression of urgency to preserve remnants of the past, accumulating them in personal, historical, and public archives. This is an expression of the "obsession with memory" and the memorializing spirit that are discussed by Nora, Gillis, and Huyssen.

There is also the type of forgetting that Ricoeur labels as "evasive," which involves an attempt not to recall potentially upsetting memories. This mood tends to prevail in historical periods following large social catastrophes, massacres, and genocides, which may engender among those who suffered them directly and survived them the desire to not know, to avoid painful remembrances as a means to continue living.

At this point, silence comes in, as the counterpart of oblivion. There are silences imposed by fear of repression in dictatorships of every stripe. Silences kept during Franco's Spain, the Stalinist Soviet Union, and the Latin American dictatorships burst open with the change of regime. During these repressive periods, painful memories survive that "await the propitious moment to be expressed" (Pollak 1989, 5). Yet the silencing of dissident memories does not have as a point of reference only a dominant dictatorial state. They also arise in the context of more horizontal relationships among social groups. Pollak (1989) analyzes several types of silences among Holocaust survivors, from those who returned to their places of origin and needed to find a modus vivendi with their neighbors who "in the form of tacit consent witnessed their deportation," to the silences about extreme situations in the camps, maintained to avoid the well-known mechanism of blaming the victims (6). There is also the will to silence, of not telling or transmitting, of keeping the traces enclosed in inaccessible spaces, in order to care for the others as an expression of the desire to not hurt them nor to convey a message of suffering.

Other silences follow a different logic. To communicate suffering and painful events, one has to find a willingness to listen and understand on the other side (Laub 1992b; Pollak 1990). At the level of individual memories, the fear of not being understood creates silences, and thus the importance of an attentive ear, of finding others with the capacity to listen. We will return to this issue in the context of personal testimonies. At the societal level, there are conjunctures of political transition—such as Chile at the end of the 1980s, or postwar France—in which the desire for reconstruction is experienced as contradictory to messages linked to the horrors of the past.[9]

Finally, there is the liberating type of forgetting, one through which the person or group feels itself free from the burden of the past, allowing a shift of focus toward the future. This is the "necessary" forgetting in the life of the individual. For communities and groups, the modern origin of these thoughts can be traced to Nietzsche, who condemns the historical fever and demands a forgetting that encourages living and makes it possible to see the world without being burdened by the heavy baggage of history. This historical fever, as Huyssen (2000) states,

> [s]erved to invent national traditions in Europe, to legitimize the imperial nation-states, and to give cultural coherence to conflictive societies in the throes of the Industrial Revolution and colonial expansion. (37)

As Ernest Renan (2000) suggested,

> Forgetting, and I would even say historical error, is an essential factor in the creation of a nation, which means that progress in historical studies is frequently a threat to nationality. (56)

The current fever for memorialization has other characteristics, and other dangers, as raised in the debate about the "abuses of memory," the title of the small and provocative book by Tzvetan Todorov (1998). Todorov is not campaigning against the recovery of memory; rather, he is concerned with its use by different groups who may appropriate memory to foster their own interests. The memory abuse that the author condemns is that of preserving a "literal" memory in which the crimes are viewed as unique and unrepeatable. In that case, the experience is not transferable; it does not lead anywhere beyond itself. Todorov defends an "exemplary" use of memory, in which the memory of a past event is conceived as one instance of a more general category, or as a model for understanding new situations with different agents. In terms of forgetting, this proposal entails the (political) forgetting of what is singular and unique about an experience in order to make memory more productive. We will take up this issue again in the next chapter.

Discourse and Experience

Let's return to the central issue that animates this inquiry, namely that of memory as the process of giving meaning to the past. Several questions can be raised here. Who is to create and convey meanings? Which is the past that is being referred to? They are active agents who remember, individuals and groups who assign meanings to the past and who often try to convey their message to others (and even impose it). This characterization must be accompanied by the recognition of the plurality of "others" and the complex dynamic of the relationship between the subject and alterity.

Which past is the one that the subject is to make significant? There are autobiographical pasts, experiences lived "in one's own skin." For those who lived through an event or experience, having done so may turn out to be a key marker in their lives and memory. If the event was a traumatic one, rather than remembrances and meaningful memories, the subject will be faced with voids, vacuum, silences, and the traces of trauma, expressed in his or her current behavior, including pathological symptoms (and, in the least frequent cases, plain "forgetting").

There are also those who did not have the "past experience" themselves. This lack of experience puts them in another category: they are "others." For this group, memory is a *representation of the past constructed as cultural knowledge shared by successive generations and by different "others."* In fact, the presence of this otherness involves thinking about experience or memory in its intersubjective and social dimensions. As Luisa Passerini argues, memories are connected one to the other.[10] Subjects can develop narrative memories because others had done it before, others who had been able to transmit and engage a dialogue about them.

Similarly, social forgetting is also intersubjective:

> What we call "forgetting" in a collective sense occurs when human groups fail—whether purposely or passively, out of rebellion, indifference, or indolence, or as the result of some disruptive historical catastrophe—to transmit what they know out of the past to their posterity. (Yerushalmi 1996, 109)

As already mentioned, these catastrophes can involve a rupture between individual memory and public and collective practices. This happens when, due to political conditions, collective practices are dominated by ritualization, repetition, deformation or distortion, silence or lies.

They can also involve silences and fault lines in the processes of inter-generational transmission.

Let me return for a moment to the difference between social memory and personal recollection and forgetting of events lived through personally. What is firsthand "experience"? In the language of common sense, experience refers to events and occurrences that are lived directly, firsthand, captured subjectively in their immediacy. Analysis of the concept of "experience" indicates, however, that it is not so directly and linearly dependent on the event or occurrence. Rather, to have an experience implies the mediation of language and the cultural interpretive framework that allow it to be expressed, to be thought about and conceptualized (Joan Scott 1992; van Alphen 1999). In fact, the central place of language for memories had already been recognized by Halbwachs. In a seldom quoted paragraph, Halbwachs (1992) points out that "[t]here are no recollections to which words cannot be made to correspond. We speak of our recollections before calling them to mind. It is language, and the whole system of social conventions attached to it, that allows us at every moment to reconstruct our past" (173). In turn, the unavoidable and ever present linguistic and narrative mediation implies that under all conditions and whatever their content, all memories—even the most individual and private ones—are socially and symbolically constituted (Ricoeur 1999).

In broader terms, this perspective suggests that the availability of symbolic tools (culture, language) is a precondition for the process of structuring subjectivity. However, the process is not simple or linear. To the contrary, as Joan Scott (1992) points out, subjects and subjectivity are constituted discursively in scenarios that imply multiple and contradictory discursive systems. In addition, subjects are not passive receivers but rather social agents with the ability to respond and transform what is conveyed to them. It could be argued, in fact, that subjectivity emerges and reveals itself in full force in the cracks, in the confusion, in the disruptions in the functioning of habitual memory, in the unrest that stimulates the person to engage in interpretive work in order to find meaning and the words with which to express it. In situations of extreme disruption and bewilderment, words to express and represent the events cannot be found, and we are faced then with the signs of trauma.

If the preceding discussion is not qualified, the reader could come to the conclusion that the perspective adopted here centers attention exclusively on discourse, on narration, and on the "power of words." This is not the perspective that we want to advance here. The power of words is not located in the words themselves but in the authority they represent and in the power-related processes connected to the institutions that legitimate them (Bourdieu 1985).

Memory as a narrative social construction involves studying the narrator and the institutions that grant or deny power to the voice of the narrator and authorize him or her to speak, since as Pierre Bourdieu notes, the effectiveness of performative speech is proportional to the authority of the speaker. Additionally, it involves paying attention to the processes of construction of legitimate recognition, socially granted by the group to which it is directed. The reception of words and acts is not a passive process. Quite to the contrary, it is an act of recognition bestowed on whoever is undertaking the transmission (Hassoun 1996).

Thus, taking language as the point of departure, the road takes us to encounter conflicts over the representations of the past, centered on and reflecting struggles for power, legitimacy, and recognition. Such struggles involve different social actors developing strategies to "officialize" or "institutionalize" a (their own) narrative of the past. Achieving positions of authority, or assuring that the occupants of those positions adopt the desired narrative, is part of these struggles. The struggle also involves a strategy for "winning supporters," widening the circle or group that accepts and legitimizes a given narrative, incorporating it as its own or identifying with it. This issue will be taken up again when discussing institutional questions related to memories.

What has all this to do with thinking about memory?

First, it matters to have or not have words to express what has been lived through, to construct experience and subjectivity stemming from events that "bump" into us. One of the characteristics of traumatic events is the massive character of their impact, creating a gap in the capacity "to be spoken" or told about. This provokes a hole in the ability to represent symbolically the event. There are no words, and therefore there cannot be memories. Memory remains disarticulated, and only painful traces, pathologies, and silences come to the surface.

Trauma alters the temporality of other psychic processes, and memory cannot handle them. It is unable to recover, convey, or communicate that which has been lived through.

Second, if "experience" is always mediated and is never "pure" or direct, it becomes necessary to rethink the apparent distance and difference between the processes of autobiographical memory and forgetting on the one hand, and the sociocultural processes shared through the mediation of mechanisms of transmission and symbolic appropriation on the other. To transform an occurrence into "experience," even those who lived through it must find the words to convey it, locating themselves in a cultural framework that makes communication and transmission possible. Analytically, this paves the way to a reconceptualization of what in common sense is understood as "transmission," namely, the process through which a shared cultural understanding linked to a given vision of the past is constructed. Thinking about mechanisms of transmission, about inheritances and legacies, about learning and the creation of traditions becomes then a significant analytical task. (These issues will be taken up in chapter 7.)

Third, the approach taken here makes it possible to articulate individual and collective or social levels of memory and experience. Memories are simultaneously individual and social. Insofar as words and the community of discourse are collective, experience is as well. Individual lived-through occurrences are not transformed into experiences with meaning without the presence of cultural discourses, and these are always collective. At the same time, individual experience and memory do not exist in themselves; they reveal themselves, and become collective, in the act of sharing. Thus, individual experience constructs community in the shared narrative act, in narrating and listening.

Nevertheless, no linear or direct relationship between the individual and the collective is to be posed or expected. Subjective inscriptions of experience are never mirrorlike reflections of public occurrences. Thus, no "integration" or "fit" between individual and public memories, or the presence of a single memory, is to be expected. There are contradictions, tensions, silences, conflicts, gaps, and disjunctions, as well as converging points and even "integration." Social reality is complex, contradictory, and full of tensions and conflicts. Memory is no exception.

In sum, "experience" is subjectively lived, culturally shared, and "shareable." It is in human agency that the past, embodied in cultural contents (discourses in the broad sense), is activated. Memory, then, is produced whenever and wherever there are subjects who share a culture, social agents who try to "materialize" the meanings of the past in different cultural products that are conceived as, or can be converted into, "vehicles for memory," such as books, museums, monuments, films, and history books. Memory shows up also in actions and expressions that, rather than re-presenting the past, incorporate it performatively (van Alphen 1997).

Three

Political Struggles for Memory

The past is gone, it is already de-termin(at)ed; it cannot be changed. The future, by contrast, is open, uncertain, and indeterminate. What can change about the past is its *meaning,* which is subject to re-interpretations, anchored in intentions and expectations toward the future.[1] That meaning of the past is dynamic and is conveyed by social agents engaged in confrontations with opposite interpretations, other meanings, or against oblivion and silence. Actors and activists "use" the past, bringing their understandings and interpretations about it into the public sphere of debate. Their intention is to establish/convince/ transmit their narrative, so that others will accept it.

Thus, research about this issue does not consist of "dealing with social facts as things, but of analyzing how social facts become things, how and why they are solidified and endowed with durability and stability" (Pollak 1989, 4). What is involved is the study of the processes and actors that intervene in the tasks of constructing and consecrating memories. Who are these actors? Whom do they confront and with whom do they engage in dialogue in the process? Different social actors, with diverse connections to past experience—those who lived through specific periods or events and those who inherited them, those who studied them, and those who expressed them in different ways—strive to affirm the legitimacy of "their" truth. They engage in struggles for power, searching often to legitimate their current positions through claiming privileged links to the past, asserting continuities or ruptures. In these processes, agents of the state have a central role and special weight because of their power in relation to establishing and developing an "official history/memory." Thus, attention has to be placed on the conflicts and disputes over interpretations and meanings of the past, and on the process through which some narratives displace others and become hegemonic.

The Production of a National History and an Official Memory

One of the central symbolic operations in the processes of state formation—in Latin America throughout the nineteenth century, for example—was the elaboration of the "master narrative" of the nation. This involved advancing one version of history that, together with patriotic symbols, monuments, and pantheons to national heroes, could serve as a central node for identification and for anchoring national identity.

What purpose do these official memories serve? They are more or less conscious efforts to define and reinforce feelings of belonging that aim to maintain social cohesion and defend symbolic borders (Pollak 1989, 9). At the same time, they provide the reference points for framing the memories of groups and sectors within each national context.

Like all narratives, these national stories are selective. Establishing a group of heroes requires obscuring the actions of others. Emphasizing certain characteristics as indicators of heroism involves silencing others, especially the errors and missteps by those who are defined as heroes and must appear "immaculate" in that history. Once these official canonical narratives, historically linked to the process of political centralization in the process of nation-state building, are established, they come to be expressed and crystallized in the history textbooks passed on in formal education. At the same time, they become the targets of diverse efforts at reform, revisionism, and construction of alternative historical narratives. Because the master national narrative tends to be the story of the victors, there will be others who—whether in the form of private oral stories or as practices of resistance to power—will offer alternative narratives and meanings of the past, threatening the national consensus that is being imposed.[2]

If the state is strong and its policing includes control over ideas and freedom of expression in public space, alternative narratives take refuge in the world of "private memories." At times, these narratives are silenced even in the sphere of intimacy, out of shame or weakness, or they are integrated into practices of more open or clandestine resistance (James Scott 1992).

In this process of construction of the master narratives of modern nation-states, professional historians have had a central role. Official master narratives are written by professional historians whose link to power is crucial to their task. Over time, antagonistic interpretations and revisions of that memory of the nation or official historical narrative will be produced, be it as a result of open antagonisms and political struggles, of changes in social sensibilities, or of advancement in historical research itself.

The construction of official histories turns to be particularly problematic when dealing with contemporary or recent events, especially when they are marked by deep social and political conflicts. During the dictatorial periods of the twentieth century—Stalinism, Nazism, military dictatorships in Brazil, Chile, Argentina, and Uruguay, Stronism in Paraguay—public space was monopolized by a dominant political story, where the "good guys" and the "bad guys" were clearly identified. Censorship was explicit, and alternative memories could arise only underground, prohibited and clandestine, thus exacerbating the ravages of terror, fear, and traumatic lapses that generate paralysis and silence. Under such circumstances, the official stories conveyed by the representatives of the regime encountered few challenges in the public sphere.

Generally, the dictatorships' narratives present the military in the role of "saviors" of the nation from a mortal threat (in the Southern Cone in the 1970s, the threat was that of "Communism") and from the chaos created by those who try to subvert the nation. In this context, subsequent military stories may emphasize the achievements of peace (especially prominent in Argentina), of economic progress (in Brazil), or of both (Chile) (Jelin 2002b). For example, in 1974, the tenth anniversary of the coup d'état in Brazil was used as an occasion to put into circulation one exclusive story in the public sphere and the school system: the account of the economic success of the military regime—the story of the Brazilian "economic miracle." There was no mentioning of the political system or of restrictions of public liberties (Carvalho and da Silva Catela 2002). Undoubtedly, the ethical and political role and public responsibility of historians and critical intellectuals are of extraordinary significance in such periods.[3]

Political openings, thaws, liberalizations, and transitions give a boost to activities in the public sphere, so that previously censored narratives and stories can be incorporated and new ones can be generated. Such openings create a setting for new struggles over the meaning of the past, with a plurality of actors and agents who express a multiplicity of demands and claims.

The new political scenario is one of institutional change in the state and in state-society relationships. At such times, the struggle plays out between a variety of actors who claim recognition and legitimacy of their voices and demands. The memories of the oppressed and marginalized and the memories about oppression and repression—at the edge, of those who were directly affected in their physical integrity by death, forced disappearance, torture, exile, and imprisonment—emerge, usually with a double intent, that of asserting the "true" version of history based on their memories, and that of demanding justice. In such moments, memory, truth, and justice blend into each other, because the meaning of the past that is being fought about is, in fact, part and parcel of the demand for justice in the present.

These are moments in which stories and narratives that were hidden or silenced for a long time emerge into the public eye. There may be considerable public surprise at the survival (at times for decades) of memories that were silenced in the public world but were kept and transmitted in the private sphere (within family or clandestine social groups), maintained in personal intimacy, even "forgotten" in an "evasive" memory loss (because they might be forbidden, unspeakable, or shameful memories, according to Pollak 1989, 8), or buried in traumatic lapses and symptoms. These conjunctures of political and expressive aperture and "uncovering" provide clear evidence that the processes of forgetting and remembering do not respond in a simple, linear, or direct manner to the passing of chronological time.[4]

Moments of political opening involve a complex political scenario. They do not necessarily or primarily entail a binary opposition between an official history or a dominant memory articulated by the state on the one hand, and a counternarrative expressed by society on the other. Quite to the contrary, multiple social and political actors come to the scene, and they craft narratives of the past that confront each other's, and in so doing, they also convey their projects and political expectations for the future. In these conjunctures, neither is there a single voice on the part of the state. Political transition involves a transformation of the state, a new foundational moment, with new readings and meanings given to the past. At times of political opening, the state itself is crisscrossed by multiple and competing readings, reflecting the variety of meanings of the past that circulate in the societal scenario.

The Conflictive History of Memories

Controversies over the meanings of the past surface at the very moment when events are taking place. At the time of a military coup or of the invasion of a foreign country, the victors interpret their actions and resulting events in terms of their insertion in a long-term historical process. Already in the initial proclamations and in the way in which the event is presented to the general population they offer an interpretation of what is going on—generally, an image that portrays the victors as saviors. As Henry Rousso argues, "[i]f we wish to understand the configuration of a discourse about the past, it must be remembered that the discourse is being constructed ever since the initial stages of the event where it is rooted" (Rousso, in Feld 2000, 32). This discourse will be revised and resignified in subsequent periods, according to the configuration of political forces and disputes that unfold in different economic and political conjunctures.

Rousso studied the memory of Vichy in France. In 1940, De Gaulle's first speeches already declared that France (the "true" one) was not defeated, and that the Vichy regime was only a "parenthesis." Starting in 1944, a mystified memory of the war was being constructed: the French are presented as heroes of the resistance, and this vision is accompanied by trials of collaborators and by the "depuration" after the war. The first wave of trials in the postwar period centered on the crime of collaboration understood as "treason against the nation." Only in the early 1970s could the French be indicted for crimes "against humanity." The definition of the norm that had been transgressed and the interpretive framework have changed by then: crimes committed by Frenchmen who were members of French fascist organizations could then be recognized. Such crimes were then disengaged from the notion of "treason against the nation."

Rather than stress treason towards France in relationship to Germany, i.e., a nationalistic vision of the crime . . . the issue becomes understanding the degree to which the perpetrators were "fascists" and "anti-semites," incorporating thus the idea, for the most part correct, that fascism and anti-Semitism belonged to the French tradition independently of the German occupation. In the extreme, in these recent representations, the German or Nazi occupier is falling to the background, especially within the framework of the criminal trials. (Rousso, in Feld 2000, 34)

Another point stressed by Rousso is that although at the beginning the charges were pressed by the state, which at that time needed to send strong signals of its rupture with the Vichy regime, decades later the instigators of judicial action and of demands of official symbolic recognition were social actors. Former deportees and resisters acted as "militants for memory," "in the name of a *'duty to remember,'* with the objective of keeping alive memory against all forms of oblivion, which in their perspective is considered as a new crime" (Rousso, in Feld 2000, 36). The public management of memory must undoubtedly be understood in the French political context, including the emergence and popularity of right-wing (and anti-Semitic) discourses and practices, as well as in the broader European context, issues that obviously go beyond the scope of this volume.

Periods of transition of political regimes take place in scenarios of confrontation between actors with opposing political experiences and expectations. Each position involves a vision of the past and an (often implicit) agenda regarding how to deal with it in the new era, always defined as a break and as a moment of change vis-à-vis the previous regime. In the Spanish transition, the painful memories of different actors facilitated convergence and negotiation, rather than a rehashing of differences and confrontations. Paloma Aguilar Fernández (1996) argues that "the existence of a traumatic memory of the Spanish Civil War played a crucial role in the institutional design of the transition, in favoring negotiations and inspiring a conciliatory and tolerant attitude towards each other on the part of the principal actors" (56). The central hypothesis of her argument is that the memories of conflict and war played a pacifying role in the transition.

What memory? How was it constructed? "First, the existence of a collective traumatic memory of the Civil War prompted most of the actors to avoid its repetition at any price . . ." (Aguilar Fernández

1996, 57–58). During the transition, most Spaniards interpreted the brutality of the Civil War that took place forty years earlier as "collective insanity," and the principal lesson they extracted from that understanding was "never again." "Such a drama must never be repeated in Spain, and all political, social, and economic forces must contribute to this aim" (Aguilar Fernández 1996, 359). At the time of Franco's death and of political transition, the memory of the Civil War was intensely activated. The connection made between that moment and the prewar period (the Second Republic) was paramount in deterring the possibility of committing the same mistakes.[5] At the same time, the effort was to forget the animosities of the past in an intentional forgetting that would help in "retaining the lessons of history, but avoiding scrutinizing it." It was a political act of forgetting, a strategic silence that could happen while the Civil War was becoming the focus of cultural expression for filmmakers, musicians, writers, and academics.[6]

The transitions in the Southern Cone were different and distinctive. In the first place, with the exception of Paraguay and to a lesser extent Brazil, the dictatorial regimes did not last for decades. Thus, there was no generational renewal and the conflicts of the past were still part of the "lived experience" of most actors. Argentina was the case where the new regime took as its banner the redress of human rights violations during dictatorship. The brutality and immediacy of the human rights abuses led to open denunciations and the possibility of political, societal, and judicial redress. In Chile and Uruguay, amnesty laws and decrees obstructed the possibilities of judicial prosecution, while the political opening allowed for the previously censored and suppressed voices of victims and their supporters to be heard. Yet in all cases, the authoritarian voices of dictatorship and its supporters did not necessarily disappear from the public sphere of debate (Acuña and Smulovitz 1996).

Unlike France in 1945, there was no occupying army in retreat, leaving behind a political community liberated from foreign yokes. Both the dictators and the democrats were national political actors and forces, and now they faced the need to coexist within the framework of the new democratic rules. The issue of how to settle accounts with the recent past thus became the focus of disputes about political strategy. Whether to promote amnesty laws, truth commissions, trials, or reparations became political issues to be tackled in each country according to the strength of different political actors.[7] In connection with memory issues, what is peculiar to the Southern Cone countries is the strong and visible presence of the human rights movement as a political actor and as an "administrator" of memory.[8] What is also notable in the region is the continuing presence of authoritarian actors—the military and the Right (especially strong in Chile)—during the political transitions, and a highly ambiguous role of the traditional political parties (notably in Uruguay).

Memory Entrepreneurs and Their Projects

In a now classic book in North American sociology, Howard Becker offers a perspective that in its time revolutionized the thinking about social deviation. In my view, this perspective provides some clues for thinking analogically about the fields of dispute over memories and the actors who participate in them (Becker 1963). Becker argues that in the process of generating and labeling certain patterns of behavior as deviant, "[s]omeone must call the public's attention to these matters, supply the necessary push to get things done, and direct such energies as are aroused in the proper direction to get the rule created" (162). He calls this group "moral entrepreneurs," enterprising moral leaders or social agents who, often out of humanitarian motivation, mobilize their energies for the sake of a cause they strongly believe in.

I borrow here this notion of *moral entrepreneur* to use it in the field of struggles over memories, insofar as those who express themselves and seek to define the field can be portrayed as "memory entrepreneurs."[9]

The problem of how and why a certain theme becomes a public issue at a given time and place has attracted the attention of analysts in diverse fields, from those working on public policies to those searching to explain the success of a film or the failure of some initiative that was expected to attract attention and provoke debate. What is clear is that the conception and development of a public issue are processes that evolve over time and require energy and perseverance. There has to be someone who initiates, who promotes and devotes her or his energies to the desired end. These are Becker's moral entrepreneurs, broadening his concept to a variety of issues in the public sphere.

In the field we are concerned with here, that of memories of recent political violence and state terrorism in conflict-ridden political scenarios, what we should find is a struggle among "memory entrepreneurs," who seek social recognition and political legitimacy of *one* (their own) interpretation or narrative of the past. We will also find them engaged and concerned with maintaining and promoting active and visible social and political attention on their enterprise.

Who are they? What do they seek? What motivates them? At different conjunctures and times, the actors on the scene are diverse, as are their interests and strategies. With respect to the dictatorships of the Southern Cone, the human rights movement has been and continues to be a privileged actor in the political enterprise of memory. Its visibility and capacity to mobilize social support have varied across the countries in the region. In Argentina, its presence and actions have been systematic and permanent, while it has been less continuous and somewhat less significant in Chile and Uruguay. Even in these countries—and also in Brazil—there have been moments and conjunctures when societal mobilization has been very high, such as the Brazilian mobilization asking for amnesty for political prisoners and exiles in 1979, and the mobilization for the plebiscite to repeal the amnesty law in Uruguay in 1986. In all cases, the human rights movement is a heterogeneous actor that encompasses (not without tensions and conflicts) diverse experiences and multiple horizons of expectation.

The human rights movements are not alone in the public sphere. There are also entrepreneurial interests that are motivated by a mix of criteria, combining the lucrative and the moral in different ways.[10] The political Right (the Pinochet Foundation in Chile is probably the emblematic case), as well as other political groups of diverse ideological stands, also play their role and push for their interpretation of the past. Academic debates and the art world offer additional channels for expression of the "memory enterprises," making available innovative interpretive frameworks and performance opportunities.

There is one group that, without question, has a privileged role in this respect: the victims who were directly affected. In France that group could include the deportees or former resistance fighters; it could be war veterans groups (from Vietnam or the Malvinas/Falkland war) or survivors of massacres. In the countries of the Southern Cone, the most visible among the directly affected persons are the relatives of the kidnapped and disappeared (those who were clandestinely abducted, their fate never disclosed nor their bodies recovered). Their relatives— the emblematic symbol being the Mothers of Plaza de Mayo in Argentina—met with each other, organized themselves to express their grievances and their pain, and formed the backbone of the human rights movement.[11] Their demands and struggles varied from case to case and over time. During dictatorship, besides the constant search for the missing and the international denunciations, their role was to offer comfort and care to themselves and other victims. After the transition to democratic rule, they tried to influence and change the meaning and the content of the "official story" of the dictatorial period, with the explicit goal of eliminating historical distortions and to bring to light and legitimate the stories that had been in the "catacombs," hidden, censored, and silenced. They also pursued material claims and reparations, anchored in their status as victims that the state must recognize and for whom it must assume responsibility. Over time, they have developed rituals; they have promoted and participated in commemorations and have demanded symbolic signs of recognition in memorials, monuments, and museums. Other voices—that of exiles, of activists in opposition to dictatorship, of religious leaders condemning repression on humanitarian grounds, of international human rights activists, and so on—have also been heard, although center stage was occupied by those defined as "directly affected."

As a matter of fact, public and political uses of memory are embedded in the concept of "memory entrepreneurs." Following Todorov, it is useful to differentiate between "good" and "bad" uses of memory. A human group can remember an event in a *literal* or in an *exemplary* way. In the first case, what is preserved is unique; it is not transferable, it does not lead anywhere beyond itself. Otherwise, and without denying the singularity of the experience, it can be translated or turned into more generalized demands. In this case, working through analogy and generalization, the recollection turns into an example that leads to the possibility of learning something from it, and the past develops into a guide for action in the present and in the future (Todorov 1998).

In the movement from literal to exemplary memory, there is also a shift from the personal to the social and the political, leading in turn to the incorporation of institutional realms. In that vein, on the basis of the analysis of the remembrance of war situations in the twentieth century (principally in Europe), Jay Winter and Emmanuel Sivan (1999) suggest that remembering is a multifaceted negotiation that includes the presence of the state—although it is not necessarily the only actor, nor is it all-powerful. Various social groups can participate in the memory negotiations, following strategies that may be convergent or contrary to the policies of the state. These are diverse voices, and some are louder than others—silence or weakness may involve being farther away from the microphones of power, self-censorship, or a lack of moral legitimacy before others. Winter and Sivan also demonstrate that the manifest intentions of a group that remembers do not necessarily coincide with their actions. There may be actors following personal and private drives (such as remembering the death in action of a son), whose personal actions end up having unexpected and unwanted consequences for the social and political memory process. There can be times, I would add, in which there is a "saturation of memory" in the public sphere, triggering a sense of rejection or a freezing of memory, opposite to what was hoped.[12]

Some Markers of Memory: Commemorations and Sites

The role of memory entrepreneurs is central to the dynamics of the conflicts that surround public memory. An initial path to probe into conflicts about memory entails analyzing the social dynamics involved in dates, anniversaries, and commemorations. Some dates have very broad and generalized meaning in a society, like September 11 in Chile, or March 24 in Argentina, dates when the military coups took place (in 1973 and 1976). Other dates might be significant at the regional or local level, based on events that happened in specific locations and affected local populations. Finally, there are dates that gain their meaning on a more personal or private level, such as the anniversary of a disappearance, the birthday of someone who is not there anymore.

Insofar as there are different social interpretations of the past, public commemoration dates are issues around which social debate and even political conflict emerge. What date should be commemorated? Or, more to the point, who wants to commemorate what? Rarely is there social consensus on these issues. September 11 is clearly a conflictive date in Chile.[13] The same event—the military coup—is recalled and commemorated differently on the left and on the right, by the military and by the human rights groups. Furthermore, the meaning of the dates changes over time, as different visions crystallize and become institutionalized, and as new generations and new actors confer them with new meanings (Jelin 2002a).

Dates and anniversaries are conjunctures when memories are activated. The public sphere is occupied by commemoration, with shared expressions of remembrance, and with confrontations about their meanings. In personal and subjective terms, these are moments in which there is an arduous labor of memory for everybody involved, for the different factions, for the old and the young—who have lived through diverse events and experiences. Facts fall into place and gain a new (dis)order, preexisting models and blueprints break down, the voices of new and old generations are heard, asking, narrating, creating new intersubjective spaces of dialogue, sharing their understandings and codes of what has been lived through, what has been heard or over-heard, what has been silenced or omitted. Such dates are landmarks or signs, junctures when the clues as to what is taking place subjectively and at the symbolic level become more visible, when the memories of different social actors are brought up to date and become part of the "present."

Even—and perhaps particularly—in such moments and periods, not everyone shares the same memories. There are conflicting narra-tives based on ideological clashes. Furthermore, there are intercohort differences among those who experienced the repression or war at dif-ferent stages of their lives, and between them and the very young, who have no personal memories of repression. This multiplicity of memories and narratives of the past generates a peculiar dynamics in the social circulation of memories. For example, over time, March 24 has been commemorated in different ways in Argentina (Lorenz 2002). During the dictatorship (1976–83), the only public expression on that day was the "Message to the Argentine People," in which the armed forces gave their version of what they had done, emphasizing their role as saviors of a nation threatened by an enemy, "subversion." Given the repressive state and the looming fear, there were no alternative stories or activities in the public sphere in Argentina. Expressions of condem-nation of the military coup could only be aired outside the country, among exiles and the international solidarity movement. A few years later, following the defeat in the Malvinas war in 1982, official com-memorations lost their authority. The "Message" was not delivered at all in 1983, the last year before the transition.

On the other side, human rights groups developed their own conflicting version of what took place on March 24, 1976, stressing state terrorism and repression of popular demands. It was the human rights movement that occupied the public stage of commemoration beginning with the political transition in late 1983. The human rights movement could practically monopolize public spaces on that date. In fact, up until the mid-1990s, the state was absent from the scene of commemoration.

Over the years, the commemorative marches and activities evolved in their configuration and order, in the slogans and demands brought forth to the government as well as in who participated and which actors decided at a given moment *not* to show up. During the first half of the 1990s (after the setback of the presidential pardons of the convicted military officers), the human rights community was weak, and there was little commemorative activity. Beginning in 1995, however, the mood changed, and the date became a significant moment of expression of a multiplicity of actors and banners, demanding action and redress on the part of the government while at the same time linking memories of dictatorship with ongoing societal demands of various sorts (social justice, police violence, rights of minorities, demands of social policies, and so on). New participants, particularly youth, employing new forms of expression and participation (such as the emergence and growth of the association of H.I.J.O.S.—Hijos por la Identidad y la Justicia, contra el Olvido y el Silencio [Children in Search of Identity and Justice, against Oblivion and Silence]—and the participation of groups of young street musicians and dancers), reflect the process of transformation of the date and its meanings (Lorenz 2002).

This short summary shows that in Argentina, the public commemorations of March 24 have not involved open confrontations and conflict between radically different versions of the past. Those who could speak during the dictatorial period kept silent afterwards, while those who were silent occupied the public scene afterwards, when the political conditions had changed.[14] The political conflicts on how to settle accounts with the past are handled in other public scenarios, particularly in the judiciary, through the cases that are brought forth in court.

The contrast between the Argentine commemoration and the display of social and political conflict every September 11 in Chile is striking. There, the hostility between actors with opposing visions of the past and projects for the future has involved considerable violence in the streets each 11th, since the time of the dictatorship up to the present (Candina Palomer 2002; on Uruguay, see Marchesi 2002a, and on Brazil, see Carvalho and da Silva Catela 2002).

Just as there are significant dates, there are also significant sites or physical markers. What are the material objects or the sites connected with past events that are chosen by different actors to territorially inscribe memories? Usually, monuments, commemorative plaques, and other markers are the ways in which official and nonofficial actors try to convey and materialize their memories. Initiatives of this sort can at times be countered by contesting actors' attempts to erase the remnants of the past, as if by changing the form and function of a place the memory of what took place will also be erased.

Struggles over monuments and commemorations unfold openly all over the world. Each and every decision to build a monument, to set up spaces for memory in places where serious affronts to human dignity were committed (concentration and detention camps, especially), to construct museums and install commemorations is the result of the initiative and the commitment of social advocacy groups that act as memory entrepreneurs. These groups usually demand public and official recognition of these physical markers, and this societal demand may generate opposition and conflicts with those who want to erase and deny, or do not give them the priority that the promoters demand. There is also the struggle over the narrative that is going to be conveyed, over the content of the story that comes to be attached to the site.[15]

Detention camps and jails of the dictatorships are sites where repression occurred. There are cases in which the physical space has been "recovered for memory," like the Peace Park in Santiago, Chile, on the premises of what was the detention camp of Villa Grimaldi during the dictatorship (Lazzara 2003). The opposite may happen as well: projects can erase signs and destroy buildings, obliterating the materialization of the remembrances in physical markers. Such was the case with the Punta Carretas jail in Montevideo, which was turned into a modern shopping mall. Other efforts to transform sites of repression into sites of memory encounter opposition and destruction, such as the plaques and commemorative structures that were installed and then vandalized in one of the sites of repression in downtown Buenos Aires, the site of the El Atlético detention camp.[16]

These places are the actual physical spaces where dictatorial repression occurred. They are undeniable witnesses. One can try to erase them and destroy the buildings where torture and murder took place, but people's personalized memories retain the marks with their multiple meanings. What happens when an effort to physically mark the memory of the past offence in a monument fails? When memory cannot be materialized in a specific site? Administrative fiat and power cannot erase personalized memories or the public projects of active entrepreneurs. Subjects must then look for alternative channels of expression. When blocked by others, the subjectivity, desire, and will of the people fighting to materialize their memories are energized, their will to act is mobilized publicly, strength is renewed. There is no pause, no rest, because the memories have not been "deposited" in any place; they have to remain active in the hearts and minds of people.[17] The issue of transforming personal feelings, which are unique and intransferable, into collective and public meanings, remains open and active. The question here is whether it is possible to destroy what people intend to remember or perpetuate. Indeed, could it be that the silence and oblivion that are sought for by repressing commemorations have the paradoxical effect of multiplying memories, of maintaining alive the questions and the public debate around the recent past? We are faced again with the issue of the disjunctions between different social groups and their subjective feelings and timings of their memory work. This paradoxical effect of repression activating rather than covering up memories may actually take place in a "personal time" or specific biographical experience of a specific human group that lived through a given period and certain events, and cannot be transferred or transmitted in an unmediated or direct way to others who did not experience it and may not be able to understand the urgency of the claim.

Controversy and conflicts over interpretations do not necessarily calm down once the memorial, museum, or monument is constructed. The initial or official understanding of the past to be conveyed by a given site may be the one presented by the group that promoted it, or it may be a "negotiated" script. With time, and with historical, political, and cultural processes developing, there will necessarily be new processes of giving meaning to the past, with new interpretations. Thus, revisions, changes in narratives, and new conflicts over interpretations will have to arise.

An extreme case of this ongoing conflict and of changes in interpretations of the past linked to political developments is provided by Germany in the wake of reunification, especially in the former German Democratic Republic. According to Claudia Koonz (1994), the stories told to visitors at the concentration camps in East Germany when it was within the Soviet orbit emphasized three basic points: first, the responsibility of fascism and monopoly capitalism for the war crimes; second, that the German working class, led by the Communist Party and assisted by Soviet troops, bravely resisted Nazi domination; and third, that this heroic legacy is the basis for future struggles against international capitalism. There was no reference to Jews, gypsies, or other non-Marxist victims in the camps. On the Western side, the narrative was very different and even opposite.

Reunification under the control of the West German regime precipitated reactions of rejection among groups of citizens in the former German Democratic Republic, who opposed remaking their histories according to the Western mold. The "official" consensuses on both sides broke down, resulting in localized conflicts (for example, about attempts to commemorate the victims of the postwar Soviet camps that had been functioning in the same sites of the Nazi camps, or efforts toward obtaining vindication or reparations for Jewish victims). There were also protests of nearby communities that did not wish to see their area damaged by horror images, and of economic interests that sought to capitalize on horror in potentially lucrative tourist attractions. As Koonz (1994) concludes,

> The concentration camps continue to haunt the German landscape, but the categories of victimhood have expanded beyond the anti-Fascist memorialized in the East and the victims of the Holocaust mourned in the West. . . .
> The landscapes of Nazi brutality retain their power to horrify. Nazi atrocities must remain at the core of a shared public memory, even as we confront the complex heritage that shapes our post-postwar world. To accomplish this, the camp memorials must both commemorate the Soviet role in the Allied liberation of the camps and recognize that some Germans died unjustly in the "special camps." The enduring legacy of the camps, however, must be to serve as warnings *(Mahnmahler)* against all forms of political terror and racial hatred. (275)

Uses and Abuses of Memory: Ownership and the Meanings of "Us"

We return now to Todorov's distinction between "recovering" a past or its traces in the face of efforts to erase it, and the use that is made of that recovered past, that is, the role the past has and should have in the present. In the sphere of public life not all memories of the past are equally admirable. There can be gestures of vengeance; alternatively, there may be learning experiences. The question that naturally follows is whether there are ways to distinguish a priori the "good" and "bad" uses of the past (Todorov 1998, 30).

Todorov proposes the distinction between "literal" and "exemplary" memory as his point of departure. The final sentence of Koonz's work is a good example of this distinction. When she asks that the legacy of the camps serve "as warnings *(Mahnmahler)* against all forms of political terror and racial hatred," she is calling for a universalizing use of the memory of the multiple horrors of the camps, and places herself against those who wish to appropriate only one of those horrors—the Nazi horrors against Jews or against gypsies versus the Soviet horrors against Germans—which would lead to a politics of glorification of some and the infamy of others and would simultaneously create "privileged victims."

Koonz's conclusion calls for an "exemplary" memory. This position involves a dual task. First, it is necessary to overcome the pain caused by remembrance and successfully contain it so that it does not invade life completely. Second, and here we move from the private and personal level to the public realm, it is necessary to learn from it, drawing from it the lessons that would make the past the guide for action in the present and the future.

Literal memory, on the other hand, stays closed within itself. All the labors of memory are situated in direct contiguity to the past. The searches and efforts to recall will serve to identify all the people who were involved in the initial suffering, to reveal each detail of what happened, to try to understand the causes and consequences of the events, and to deepen and immerse oneself in them. But they cannot serve to guide future behavior in other areas of life, because literal memories are incommensurable, and the transmission to other experiences is impossible. Literal use, according to Todorov (1998), "makes the past event something insuperable, and ultimately makes the present subject to the past" (31).

The uses made of memory correspond to these two types. In the literal case, memory is an end in itself, in opposition to what Koonz seeks. Action is explained and justified as a "duty to remember," and there is a moral mandate to perpetuate constant recollection against all forms of forgetting. In this vein, Rousso complains of the "militants of memory," whose impact will vary according to whether the broader context will receive them more or less openly, or even refuse to listen.[18] The notion of "memory entrepreneur" developed earlier implies elaborating memories in terms of, or in view of, a project or endeavor, and this may open the possibility of moving toward an "exemplary" memory.

The public and social issues raised by these two positions directly refer to the way a political community is constituted and the rules that govern it. Allow me to introduce Guaraní at this point, since it may be helpful. In Guaraní (an indigenous language spoken on a daily basis by the Paraguayan population) there are two words to express the idea of "us." One, *ore,* marks the boundary separating the speaker and his or her community from the "other," the one who listens and observes, who clearly is excluded from the "us." The other word, *ñande,* is an inclusive "us" that invites the interlocutor to be part of the community. I want to suggest that the two types of memory, and their uses, correspond to these two notions of "us" or of community, one inclusive and the other exclusive and excluding.[19]

Practices of commemoration and the attempts to establish memory sites always involve political struggles. The principal adversaries in these conflicts are, on the one hand, the social forces that demand markers of memory and, on the other, those who seek to erase these markers on the basis of rendering a narrative of the past that minimizes or eliminates the meaning of what the others wish to remember. There are also confrontations over the "appropriate" forms or means of remembering, as well as over which actors have legitimacy to act, that is, who has the (symbolic) "truth" or the power to decide the contents of the memory to be conveyed. These conflicts can be discussed under the label of the issue of the "ownership" of memory.

At one level, there is a confrontation about the appropriate and inappropriate forms of expression. Are there standards for judging remembrances and memorials? Further, and most importantly, who is the authority that is going to decide which are the "appropriate" forms of remembering? Who embodies *true* memory? Is being a direct victim of repression a necessary condition? Can those who have not themselves lived through repression participate in the historical process of building social memory? The very definition of what constitutes "personal experience" or being a "direct victim" is also part of the historic process of social construction of meaning.

No one doubts the pain of the victim nor the victim's right to recover the truths of what took place under repressive regimes. Nor is there any question of the protagonist role (in concrete historical situations) that "direct victims" and their families took as the initial voices in the entrepreneurship of memories. The issue is a different one and, in fact, is a dual one. First, who is the "us" with legitimacy for remembering? Is it an exclusive us, in which only those who "lived through" the events can participate? Or is there room to broaden that "us," in practices through which legitimate mechanisms of incorporation begin to function for (us) others? Is it an *ore* or a *ñande*?

On the other hand, the theme posed by Todorov becomes significant. To what extent does memory serve to broaden the horizon of experiences and expectations? Or is it restricted to the event being remembered? At this point, memory comes into play in another context, that of justice and institutions. When generalization and universalization are introduced, memory and justice converge, in opposition to intentional oblivion (Yerushalmi 1996).

A preliminary hypothesis, which will have to be the focus of future research, relates the scenarios of struggles over memory to state action. When the state does not develop official and legitimate institutionalized channels that openly recognize past state violence and repression, the conflict over truth and over "proper" memories develops in the societal arena. In that scenario, there are strong voices that claim their own "truths": the discourse of direct victims and their closest relatives, and the discourse of perpetrators who "saved" the nation. In the absence of parameters for sociopolitical legitimation based on general ethical criteria (the legitimacy of the rule of law) and of the translation or transfer of memory to institutional justice, there will be ongoing disputes about who can promote or demand what, about who can speak and in whose name.

The question of the authority of memory and the *Truth* can take on an even more disquieting dimension. There is a danger of anchoring the legitimacy of those who express the *Truth* in an essentialized vision of biology and the body (a mirror image of biological racism). For many, personal suffering (especially when it was experienced directly in "your own body" or by blood-connected relatives) can turn to be the basic determinant of legitimacy and truth. Paradoxically, if legitimacy for expressing memory of a painful past is socially assigned to those who suffered repression on their own bodies or that of their kin, this symbolic authority can easily (consciously or unconsciously) slip into a monopolistic claim on the meaning and content of the memory and the truth.[20] The recognized "us" is thus exclusive and nontransferable. Furthermore, under social conditions that foster the prevalence of silence and the absence of social spaces for memory circulation (mechanisms that are needed for enabling processes of working through traumatic symptoms), victims can find themselves isolated and trapped in a ritualized repetition of their pain, without any access to the possibility of dialogue and to a friendly environment for working through their suffering. Taken to the extreme, this situation can lead to obstructing the mechanisms for broadening the social compromise with memory by not leaving room for the reinterpretation and resignification—on their own terms—of the meaning of the experiences transmitted.

The discussion of these themes presents us with a double historical danger. One danger is institutional oblivion and void, which turns memories into literal memories of nontransferable property, which cannot be shared. Under such circumstances, the possibility for incorporating new subjects is blocked. Another danger is the fixation of the "militants of memory" on the specific events of the past, which obstructs the possibility of creating new meanings. Choosing to speak of memory "entrepreneurs" injects an element of optimism here: Entrepreneurs know very well that their success depends not on mechanical reproduction but on widening scales and scopes, on their capacity to create new projects and open new spaces. It is here where the possibility of a *ñande* and of the action of exemplary memory rests.

Four

History and Social Memory

The relationship between memory and history is nowadays a central preoccupation within several fields of the social sciences. Debates and reflection on the subject are most extensive and intensive within the discipline of history itself, particularly among those scholars who, recognizing that the historian's craft extends beyond the mere "reconstruction" of what "actually" happened, deploy more complex modes of analysis in their work. An initial complexity emerges from the recognition that what "actually happened" includes the subjective perceptions and experiences of social actors. Furthermore, historical knowledge includes interpretive processes, the construction and selection of the "facts," and the selection of narrative strategies on the part of the historian.[1]

Reflection about temporality, the past, memory, and processes of social change is also taking place in other fields, ranging from philosophy to ethnography. There are, at this point, three ways in which to think about the possible relationships between history and memory: first, there is memory as a resource for research—as part of the process of obtaining and constructing "data" about the past; second, there is the role that historiographic research can play in the "correction" of false or equivocal memories; and finally, there is memory as an object of research itself.

Memory in Social Research

Within the tradition of the social sciences (including history), appeals to memory have been ubiquitously present in the process of collecting and constructing "data." When data-gathering techniques are utilized—in surveys that usually ask for some retrospective information such as place of birth, in life history interviews, or in analyses based on secondary sources (such as autobiographies, memoirs, and other kinds of life historical narratives)—the "data" presuppose the intervention and mediation of subjects that remember, register, and transmit these recollections. This process also involves the participation of the subjects who ask and organize the questions being asked and, in doing so, establish the frameworks through which the events or processes will be narrated and conveyed. In this sense, every question or interrogation becomes a mechanism of "normalization," insofar as it necessarily imposes the categories with which a powerful interrogating subject will "register" what is gathered.[2]

Traditionally, this process of recollection and the important mediating role played by subjectivity have posed a number of technical and methodological questions about the reliability or trustworthiness of the information gathered through these strategies. The problem lies in the fact that there may very well be "errors"—both voluntary and involuntary—in particular recollections and in their transmission, including lapses and other "tricks" of the unconscious. Concerns over the authenticity and sincerity of mnemonic narratives emerge from precisely such phenomena, leading researchers to introduce control questions and other methodological mechanisms to safeguard the veracity of their data and to approximate, as closely as possible, these recollections to what actually happened. At the extreme, these concerns can lead to an opposition between history and memory, in which the former is taken to be constituted by scientifically verifiable facts—what actually happened (LaCapra 1998, 16)—and the latter is relegated to the sphere of uncritical belief, myth, and the "invention" of the past, often with an idealized or romanticized version of that past. These understandings explain the misgivings, discomfort, and nervousness expressed by many historians vis-à-vis the growing scholarly interest in memory.

Yet the current preoccupation with memory is much more varied and conceptually complex than the positivistic dichotomy between fact and belief might lead us to believe. We are witnessing a proliferation of studies, conferences, and debates about memory, and this is linked to epochal transformations, to ongoing sociocultural processes, and to concomitant changes in dominant social scientific frameworks. While in the cultural sphere we are seeing an "explosion of memory," paradigmatic shifts within the social sciences over the past decades have led to a growing interest and emphasis on the transformations of subjectivity, on the meanings of social action, and on introducing in the analysis the perspective of social actors themselves. These shifts are evident in a number of disciplines and fields, ranging from sociology, ethnography, and ethnohistory to historiographic research on *mentalités* and on the processes that constitute everyday life.

Such scholarly interests in subjectivity, the construction of social identities in the context of meaningful action, and the active and productive role of individual and collective subjects (the issue of agency) reveal themselves in the attention paid to the study of social processes that involve changes normally accompanied by the subjects' reflexivity—migration, the family, sexuality, changing practices in the face of new technologies, and so on. These preoccupations are also visible, and significantly so, in current thinking and debate over the ways in which meaning is itself constructed in the research process. For radical positivists, what is "factual" is that which is linked to the existence of material evidence that something took place, irrespective of the subjectivity of the actors involved (including their beliefs, emotions, and desires). Such a perspective inevitably excludes the consideration of memory. A radical constructivist perspective, on the other hand, may lead to privileging subjective narratives to such a degree that memory (including possible fictionalizations and mythifications) ends up being identified with and collapsed into "history" (LaCapra 1998, 16; LaCapra 2001, chapter 1).[3]

The exploration we want to embark on here requires us to take a step further, perhaps even two. It is not only the task of posing a counterpoint or a relation of complementarity between "hard data" (coming from critically assessed documents and other sources) and "soft data," such as the subjective perceptions and beliefs of actors and witnesses. The events that interest us here have a further characteristic that complicates the analysis. As already mentioned, memory-oblivion, commemoration, and recollection become crucial when they refer to traumatic events such as political repression and extermination, when what is in question involves profound social catastrophes and situations of collective suffering. It is in relation to such experiences and particularly in the context of the political and scholarly debates about the Shoah that the links and tensions between history and memory have acquired a growing salience in intellectual discussions and in scholarly debates.

Furthermore, examining the meanings of the past and their incorporation into contemporary political struggles raises the issue of the relationship between memories and "historical truths." Historiographic debate on the matter is primarily focused on the various attempts to legitimate oral history within the discipline and around notions of history as a constructed narrative. This is an "internal" debate, taking place inside history and other social science disciplines. Yet this debate can also have public and political dimensions, particularly in the context of politically conflictive issues. In effect, the historian or social scientist may under certain conditions become a public actor, and his or her positions vis-à-vis a particular conflict may have political consequences that extend beyond disciplinary knowledge and academic debate. These are conjunctures in which "the historians" decide or are called to intervene in the public sphere in response to the political and ideological controversies raised in contemporary political struggles. The Manifesto published by Chilean historians,[4] the debates among German historians, and the willingness (or refusal) of scholars to participate as expert witnesses in judicial proceedings (Rousso 2002) are all examples of this kind of political scenario where scholars are called to intervene in settling confrontations between "false" or distorted renderings of the past and "historical truths."

These cases are examples of the convergence or clash between social memory and oblivion on the one hand, and scholars working in the academic discipline of history (and related fields) on the other, in one specific arena—that of civic public action, which is anchored in ethical and moral commitments. As Yosef Yerushalmi points out, one of the tasks of the professional historian is to rescue the past, which is rarely recognizable in tradition or in societal memory (and which, according to the author, are in the process of extinction). Claiming the labor of history as that of "correcting" memories is, in this case, a central component of the professional commitment of the professional historian, in his or her dual responsibility as a researcher and a citizen. History—and by extension, social research more broadly—has therefore the role of producing critical knowledge that may then gain political significance.

Nevertheless, there is something more, or perhaps something different, present in the tasks of social research. Both radical positivism and radical constructionism deploy discourses that seek closure, in other words, a definitive answer that approximates "truth." Yet with respect to the issues that concern us here—characterized as they are by traumas and ambiguities, silences and excesses, by the search for objectivity combined with ethical and affective commitments—the tasks of search and research, as LaCapra (2001) argues, may perhaps be situated in a "third position":

> . . . the position I defend puts forth a conception of history as tensely involving both an objective (not objectivist) reconstruction of the past and a dialogic exchange with it and other inquirers into it wherein knowledge involves not only the processing of information but also affect, empathy and questions of value. (35)

Trauma, Social Catastrophe, and Historical Memory

When memory is taken up as an object of study, the relationship between memory and history takes on another significance, particularly when issues related to trauma are introduced as a dimension for analysis. Intense traumatic events generate in the subject who lives through them an inability to respond, leading to diverse kinds of difficulties in the ability to function socially. As Susana Kaufman (1998) points out,

> At the time of the event, because of the suddenness and intensity of its impact, something becomes detached from the symbolic world, and remains without representation. From that moment on, the event will not be felt as one belonging to the subject. It will remain foreign to him or her, and it will be difficult or impossible to talk about it. The event will not be integrated into the experience of the subject and its effects will be displaced to other spaces that the subject cannot control. The intensity of the event produces a breakdown in comprehension, opening a breach or a void in the subject's ability to explain what has occurred. (7)

The traumatic event is repressed or denied and is only registered later, after some time has passed, through the appearance of a variety of symptoms. Once again, this time in the context of individual and intersubjective processes, we are faced with evidence that the temporality of social phenomena is not linear or chronological but is characterized by breaches, ruptures, and the repetition of symptoms that do not fade or become diluted with the mere passage of time (Caruth 1995).

In the many places that have experienced war, violent political conflicts, genocide, and repression—situations of social catastrophe and collective trauma—the processes of expressing and making public the interpretations and meanings of those pasts are extremely dynamic, as these interpretations and meanings are never fixed once and for all. They change over time, following a complex logic that combines the temporality of the expression and of the working through and acting out of trauma (be it as symptoms or as "breakthroughs," as silences or as regaining lost memories), the explicit political strategies of various actors, and the questions, answers, and conversations introduced in the public sphere by younger generations.

The relationship between traumatic events and the temporal processes that follow, including silences and lapses, has traditionally been a center of attention of psychologists and clinical workers (Heimannsberg and Schmidt 1993). It has come to be a focus of attention in efforts of other disciplines to understand the ways in which the past emerges actualized in the present or is understood as memory and recollection in narrative or performance (LaCapra 1998, 2001; Brison 2002; van Alphen 1997). At this juncture it is important to revisit a paradox of memory that was briefly touched on in chapter 1: the acting-out of trauma, which almost always involves the repetition of symptoms, the return of the repressed or ritualized reiteration, can in many cases become the basis of identity. This generates a fixation with and in that past, which may be accompanied by fear and reticence regarding change and the possible elaboration of trauma. Such possibility of leaving behind the past (of working through trauma) may come to signify a kind of betrayal of the memory of what has taken place and of the past more generally. Working through traumatic events requires establishing a certain distance between past and present in order to be able to remember that something happened in that past and is not the present. At the same time, it requires the recognition of current life conditions and the possibility of imagining a future. In memory, in contrast to traumatic repetition, the past does not invade the present, it informs it.

Historicizing Memory

Changing political scenarios, the emergence of new social actors, and the transformation of social sensibilities inevitably bring about transformations in the meanings of the past. Examples of such changes are numerous. These are not necessarily exercises in negation or denial (although these no doubt exist) but rather processes of change in the selectivity through which diverse social actors emphasize, privilege, and reclaim particular aspects or dimensions of the past, and in the emotional and affective investments involved in the past. Therefore, the construction of memories of the past becomes an object of study for history itself, the historical study of memory, which demands the "historicization of memory."

The significance of past events is never constant or immutable; their meanings are never established once and for all. Furthermore, the relationship between the salience of a particular event and the passing of chronological time is never linear and direct, in the sense that the memory of an event would necessarily fade with passage of time to be replaced by other temporally more proximate ones. These complexities suggest that the historical dynamics of memory need to be problematized and studied. The social location of diverse social actors and their sensibilities and dispositions, the particularities of the political arena that they inhabit, and the struggles over meaning in which they are involved are some of the elements that help us to make sense of these meanings in flux. This is an explicit objective in the works of Henry Rousso about the memory of Vichy France, in which he demonstrates how with the passage of time, different social and political actors selectively recuperate particular events and particular characteristics of the period (Rousso 1990; Conan and Rousso 1994). He writes that "the issue with memory is not that there is an event about which part of the truth is revealed immediately, and much more of it fifty years later. No, it is the configuration that changes" (in Feld 2000, 35).

This analytical strategy is also present in Paloma Aguilar Fernández's work about the memory of the Spanish Civil War, in which she analyzes in detail the evolution of official discourses about the war during both the Franco period and the transition to democracy. In this case, the conceptual challenge the author confronts is how to overcome the dilemma between "presentism" (which claims that the past is continually modified at the service of the interests of the present) and "taxidermism" (which emphasizes the reproduction of the past on the premise that are not limitless to the possibilities of manipulating the past). She resolves this dilemma by highlighting the political lessons—which in the Spanish case are fundamentally negative—that diverse political actors drew from the memories of the war to confront the uncertainties of the democratic transition (Aguilar Fernández 1996).

The history of the resignifications of the Nazi period and of the genocides committed by Germany, much like the meanings that the Nazis' extermination policies have acquired in different places and times, could certainly fill entire libraries.[5] The significance ascribed to the Shoah, both in the past and the present, in Germany, in Israel, in the United States, and in other places in the world, has changed with the passage of time, gaining its meaning as part of specific political (and economic) tensions and conflicts.

In the case of the Argentine military dictatorship (1976–83), the emphases on what to remember and what to highlight have changed over time. During the dictatorship itself, the human rights movement, both within the country and within the broader international solidarity network, constructed a narrative centered around the value of human rights and the violations committed by the military regime (and by the preexisting paramilitary forces of the Argentine Anticommunist Alliance). The emblematic figure of state terrorism during that period was that of the forcefully detained disappeared person, seen as a victim of the unimaginable—so unimaginable in fact that it took considerable time to construct this figure, since there was always the hope that the authorities would recognize that a prisoner was in their custody and, in effect, make him or her reappear (Jelin 1995; for the figure of the "disappeared," see García Castro 2000, 2001).

From the perspective of the armed forces, the enemy that was constructed was "subversion," an evil figure that through armed struggle and its ideological offensive sought to question the very foundations of the nation. Military discourse was the discourse of war, and as would become evident later, this was going to be a "dirty" war (Acuña and Smulovitz 1995, González Bombal 1991). At the time of transition in 1983, the human rights language and discourse became the "foundational ethics" of the new regime (González Bombal 1992). For the interpretive framework of human rights violations, the polarity is between human rights violators on one side and victims on the other. In the initial phase of the transition, the dominant discourse was exactly that one, which meant silencing the militancy of many of the disappeared and the political conflicts and the armed struggle that immediately preceded dictatorship. The dominant image was of an "innocent" victim, grabbed away from normal life by state terrorism (on views of relatives, see da Silva Catela 2001).

These contrasting images of the military and the human rights movement at the time of transition gave way soon to significant shifts in the discourses and institutional practices of the state. On the one hand, the transition government constructed an interpretation based on a scenario in which two violent forces were confronting each other (the "two demons"), while the population at large, the "good citizens" who favored peace and democracy, were caught in the middle, unarmed and defenseless. The "silent majority" was allegedly external to and absent from these struggles, suffering the consequences of the conflict rather than being an active participant in the confrontation. This middle ground enabled this alleged majority to identify itself with the notion that *"por algo será"* (there must be a reason for repression)—a position that implicitly justified the repressive acts of the military regime. On the other hand, the accusations against and the judicial prosecution of the former commanders of the armed forces (in the 1985 trial) strengthened the figure of the "victim" of state repression as the central figure of the period, regardless of his or her ideology or actions. A victim is a passive being, harmed by the actions of others. The victim is never an agent, never productive. He or she receives blows but is construed as incapable of provoking or responding.

The 1985 trial of the former military commanders of the dictatorial juntas offered a suitable context for the depoliticization of the conflicts. The formal juridical framework eliminated all references to ideologies and political commitments of the victims. The objective was to determine that crimes had been committed, without asking about— and explicitly omitting—the possibility of political motives behind the actions of both victims and perpetrators.[6] During the trial, the image of the victim was instrumental in establishing and reinforcing the culpability of the perpetrators without mitigating circumstances or justification. A question that remains for future research is the extent to which the judicialization of a particular conflict, like the violent political conflict of the 1970s in Argentina, leads to its depoliticization, particularly in instances where the narrative of past atrocities is framed in penal rather than political discourse.[7]

Later on, once the state had recognized the legitimacy of the claims regarding human rights violations and a juridically recognized "truth" had been established, the country entered a new phase. There were several military threats and uprisings in an attempt to halt further indictments and trials, leading to laws and presidential decisions to limit the judicial route to handle past violations (Acuña and Smulovitz 1995). Notwithstanding these institutional developments, from different societal positions and perspectives diverse initiatives began to emerge to recuperate not only the memories of human rights violations but the memories of political militancy and activism as well. Numerous social actors participated in this process, with diverse aims and objectives. Current and former activists offered their testimony and interpretations about periods of conflict in the recent past, as part of the societal need to remember or as part of the "memory enterprise." Some political movements referred to a past of protest and militancy to demonstrate historical continuities in the country's social and political struggles. Young people who had not lived through the period of repression brought new kinds of questions to the public fore: some approached the past "naively," asking fresh questions or entering into dialogue without the preconceptions and prejudices of the time; many others brought to bear their histories of familial suffering and loss, transmitted through complex intergenerational identifications. In the 1990s, the political scenario had changed, and the issues and questions raised were new and renewed.

These examples, touched on only briefly, refer to public arenas and prevailing images in specific places and at specific times. They demonstrate with utmost clarity something that was discussed earlier in this book and will return throughout: that the temporality of memories is not linear, chronological, or rational. Historical processes linked to the memories of conflictive pasts have moments of greater visibility and moments of latency, of apparent oblivion or silence. There are also transformations in the content of what is selected as the key elements of the past, and the "use" made of the past and of history (Traverso 2001). When new actors enter the public stage or new political circumstances surface, preexisting interpretations of given periods or events of the past are resignified and may acquire an unexpected degree of public visibility.[8]

Furthermore, these processes are affected in significant ways by the processes and transformations of subjectivity, so significantly marked by the manifestations and elaborations over time of traumatic events and traces. To incorporate the analysis of subjectivity and symbolic manifestations into the focus of attention of the social sciences requires that these "memories" and lapses, as well as the timing of their appearance or eruption, be dealt with in depth. In such an analytical framework, special attention has to be placed on the relationship between past events and their effects, "residues" and legacies in later historical periods. Therefore, memories become a significant object of study, calling for rigorous inquiry into the links between past histories and present memories, both in terms of what is remembered and silenced and the specific mechanisms through which diverse actors remember and forget, particularly in the face of social catastrophes, because "what is denied or repressed in a lapse of memory does not disappear; it returns in a transformed, at times disfigured and disguised manner" (LaCapra 1998, 10).

The paradox is that the traumatic voids are at the same time part of what is to be understood and narrated as part of the past, and "black boxes" that hinder the very possibility of elaborating such a narrative. As LaCapra rightly states, "The traumatic event has its greatest and most clearly unjustifiable effect on the victim, but in different ways it also affects everyone who comes in contact with it: perpetrator, collaborator, bystander, resister, those born later" (LaCapra 1998, 8–9).

The Rifts between History and Memory

In sum, there is no one unique way to articulate the relationship between history and memory. Multiple levels and diverse kinds of relationships are present. Memory is by no means identical to history. Yet memory is a crucial source of history, and this includes particularly the distortions, displacements, and negations that characterize it, thus bringing up analytical enigmas and issues that call for further research. In this sense, memory functions as a stimulus for the development of the agenda for historical research. History, on the other hand, allows us to probe and critically question the contents of memory, and this helps in the task of narrating and transmitting critically established societal memories.

There is more to be said about memory when it is converted into the focus of study, objectified as a historical event. "The relevant historical event is not what actually happened, but the *memory* of the event," writes Alessandro Portelli (1989) as the final sentence of his study on the memories of the death of Luigi Trastulli. Why, asks Portelli, do people make a temporal displacement, situating the death of Trastulli in the 1952–53 protests surrounding a wave of layoffs rather than in the 1949 protests against NATO, when it actually happened? He finds an answer to this apparent "error" in the narratives of witnesses in the changing social and political climate in Italy during those years.

The 1944 massacre at the Fosse Ardeatine in Rome, another important memory-event, was a reprisal on the part of the occupying German forces for an attack carried out by the Italian resistance in central Rome. Thirty-three German police officers died in the attack. In less than twenty-four hours, German occupation forces—following their "ten for one" policy—rounded up 335 locals of diverse socioeconomic and ideological backgrounds and executed them on the outskirts of the city at the Fosse Ardeatine. There should have been 330, but the German troops made a mistake during their roundups in the city and decided to execute all the prisoners anyway. This event gained notoriety in the late 1990s when Erich Pribke, a Nazi officer, was extradited from Bariloche, Argentina, to Italy, where he was tried and condemned to a life sentence for his participation in the massacre (Portelli 1999).

When Portelli asked witnesses and Roman bystanders how much time elapsed between the original attack and the German reprisal, the majority of his informants—regardless of their age, political affiliation, and educational level—replied that the reprisal had come anywhere from three days to one year after the attack, when in fact only twenty-four hours elapsed between the two events. Why, Portelli asks, has such a strong narrative been constructed about the time lapse between the action of the resistance and the German reprisal at the Fosse Ardeatine? In fact, the belief is so strong that it may be considered a myth, impermeable to factual documentation. Extending the time between the two events opens the possibility for reaffirming the belief that the Germans first demanded the surrender of the Italians partisans that had carried out the attack, warning that retaliation would follow if they failed to do so. In this line of thought, the reprisal followed the lack of response on the part of the partisans in the time provided. This belief, however, has no basis in truth. Yet it continues to have hold of the Roman population, and it keeps being conveyed.

The search for an explanation for this temporal hiatus and this belief leads Portelli to inquire about the ideological frameworks within which both dominant and subaltern memories have been articulated in postwar Italy. What is most important within these narratives is the stereotypical construction of the German character (defining them as "brutal" relieves them of moral responsibility), and responsibility is then ascribed to the Italian resistance movement. In the popular imagination, the line goes: if the partisans had only turned themselves in . . .

In this case, this history of memory is mediated by the changing perceptions of the Italian resistance movement over time. It was easy to assimilate its combined role as hero and victim, fighting to save the nation and perishing in that fight. But its role in the Roman attack in Via Veneto was different. The partisans played an active role that resulted in death (including "innocent" deaths of bystanders).[9] For the Italian common sense, it was easier to take this attack as an isolated incident for which the partisans could be held responsible, taking it out of the historical context of the war, than to revise the clear-cut images and incorporate the ambivalences and ambiguities regarding the war actions of the partisans.

The model used by Portelli in these research projects may illustrate the diverse and multiple levels of the relationship between history and memory. Portelli locates his central research questions in the hiatus, the lapse, and the distance between "History"—the painful events that took place in a specific place and time—and the ways in which participants and neighbors narrate, remember, and symbolically represent these events. The point here is not to uncover and denounce "false memories" or to analyze symbolic representations in and by themselves but to understand the fractures and lapses between the two and between the multiple narratives that are constructed around a particular event over time. There is a multiplicity of narratives about a past event, ranging from bureaucratic and journalistic accounts to the more intimate and personalized testimonies of relatives of the victims, narratives that refer to the past but are integrated into the temporality of the moment of narration. This multiplicity allows the author to incorporate the complexity of the various levels (ethical/political, collective action, personal feelings) in the analysis of the mechanisms through which time is de-composed and rearranged in the workings of subjectivity. It also allows the author to link subjectivity to the interpretive frameworks available at different moments (in his analysis, these are located primarily within the political frameworks of the narratives of the Italian Left and the Italian Right) and to how these change over time. In this way, the "hard," fact-based history of events that actually took place becomes an indispensable component, yet one that is not sufficient in itself, for understanding the ways in which social subjects construct their memories, their narratives, and their various and at times conflictive interpretations of the events.

From such a perspective, history does not dissolve itself within memory—as radical subjectivism and constructivism would contend—nor is memory something to be ignored as data or fact because of its "volatility" or its lack of "objectivity." It is in the tension and the cracks between one and the other where the most creative, provocative, and productive questions for inquiry and critical reflection emerge.

Five

Trauma, Testimony, and "Truth"

I start to doubt the possibility of telling the story. Not that what we
lived through is indescribable. It was unbearable.
                                   Jorge Semprún, *Literature or Life*

What can people who lived through "unbearable" situations say or tell
about them? What ethical, political, and more generally human issues
are involved? Debates about testimony pervade practically every disciplinary field, from literary criticism to the broader area of cultural
critique, from philosophy to history, from political studies to psychoanalysis, sociology, and anthropology.

Testimony after Auschwitz

Reflection and debate about the possibility and impossibility of bearing testimony, about the "truth," the silences and lapses, and about
the possibility of listening owe their origin and force in contemporary
times to the Nazi experience and the debates that it has engendered.
The abundant literature about the victims of Nazism and the avatars
of their personal narratives and testimonies offer a vast array of argu-
ments and several lines of debate that can be of help in understanding
and questioning the issues involved in personal testimony after living
through extreme or limit conditions (Wieviorka 1998, 1999).

In fact, there are a number of separate but interrelated issues involved. The first refers to the obstacles and hindrances to the production of testimonies, to the possibility that those who lived through and survived extreme situations could talk about what they lived through. The impossibility of constructing a narrative and the symbolic lapses and voids involved in trauma are relevant in this issue. Yet it also involves deliberate silence, as the "foremost indicator of the dual extreme or limit character of the concentrational experience: the limit of the possible and, for this very reason, the limit of what is speakable" (Pollak 1990, 12).[1] The second issue involves the testimonial itself, the voids and lapses that characterize it, what can and cannot be said, and what makes or does not make sense for both the person narrating and the listeners. Finally, there is the issue of the uses, effects, and impacts of testimonials on society and the social setting at the moment in which they are narrated. Also involved is the issue of the appropriations and meanings that diverse audiences may ascribe to the testimonial over time.

The suffering involved in the limit situation of the concentration camp, the attempt of the Nazis (successful at its time) to negate the humanity of the victims and reduce them to an animal condition, are well known at this point in history. They have been portrayed through innumerable forms and vehicles—history books, photography, film, literature, theater, art, and the testimonials of survivors.

In all these cases, the point of departure is the testimonial marks born by survivors. There are two meanings to the word *witness* that come into play here. First, a witness is a person who lived through an experience or event and can, at a later moment, narrate it or "give testimony." This is testimony in the first person, insofar as the narrator lived through what he or she is attempting to narrate. The notion of *witness* also denotes an observer, someone who was present at the moment of an event as an onlooker, who saw something but who did not participate directly or was not directly involved in the event. His or her testimony can be used to verify that the event actually occurred.

In the first case, that of the witness-as-participant, there are events and experiences that cannot be accessed through testimonial narratives, since there are no survivors. No one has returned from the gas chamber, just as no one has returned from the "death flights" in Argentina (Verbitsky 1995), to tell their experience or even to silence their own trauma. This black hole in personal life, this historical void, signals an absolute limit of the ability to narrate. Here is the void and the human impossibility discussed by Primo Levi, who then recognizes in himself the second notion of the witness, the "duty to remember," to testify "in the name of others," as a "delegative" narrator. This is a duty that falls upon survivors. The witness-participant that cannot bear testimony, in the world of the concentration camps and particularly at Auschwitz, takes on the figure of the "Musselmann"—the person who loses his human condition before his or her physical death:[2]

> . . . we, the survivors, are not the true witnesses. . . . The destruction brought to an end, the job completed, was not told by anyone, just as no one ever returned to describe his own death. Even if they had paper and pen, the drowned would not have testified because their death had begun before that of their body. Weeks and months before being snuffed out, they had already lost the ability to observe, to remember, to compare and express themselves. We speak in their stead, by proxy. (Levi 1988, 83–84)

The survivors can speak about what they saw. Yet they also "lived" in the concentration camp themselves, although not reaching the extreme condition from which there is no return. Therefore, survivors can bear testimony as observers of what happened to others and, at the same time, bear witness of their own experiences and of the events in which they participated.

Those who lived the experience of the concentration camp and of persecution can have very vivid and detailed memories of what transpired—of the thoughts and the feelings that accompanied the events they lived through.[3] Many felt an overwhelming need to repeatedly and constantly narrate their experiences. Levi (1988) mentions this difference: "Those who experienced imprisonment . . . are divided into two distinct categories, . . . those who remain silent and those who speak. . . . I am not one of the taciturn" (149–50). Jorge Semprún, who was an inmate in Buchenwald, did write about his detention after being released, but he was among those who did not speak of the life in the camp itself until fifty years later (Semprún 1997). Thus, some felt the imperative to tell their story, as if it were a means of survival, while others felt that they needed to survive the horror in order to be able to tell the story. However, the overwhelming need to narrate can also be insatiable, and the subject may always feel betrayed by the lack of adequate words or the insufficiency of symbolic vehicles to convey his or her life story.

The need to narrate can also fall into silence, into an impossibility of telling the story, due to the lack of open ears and hearts of people willing to listen. In that case, there is no choice but to remain silent, to keep to oneself, or attempt to forget. Those who opt for that silence, however, do not necessarily find peace and calm in their life. "The 'not telling' of the story serves as a perpetuation of its tyranny" (Laub 1992a, 79) and often provokes deep distortions in memory and in the organization of everyday life later on. In the extreme, the witness becomes trapped in an irresolvable situation. Either he or she tells his or her story, running the risk of losing the audience that may not want or may not be able to listen to everything he or she has to say, or he or she remains silent in order to preserve the relationship to that audience, at the cost of perpetuating the communicative void.

According to Dori Laub, at a more general historical level, the Nazi extermination succeeded at the time it was taking place, becoming an event without witnesses. There could be neither internal witnesses—their capacity to bear witness being annihilated in the ultimate or extreme figure of the "Musselmann"—nor external ones. There were some people in the ghettos and the camps who perceived and denounced what was happening, people who buried their diaries and other writings.[4] What was missing was the human capacity to perceive, assimilate, and interpret what was going on. The outside world was not able to recognize it, and therefore nobody took the place of the observer/witness of what was taking place. One could argue that the available cultural interpretive frameworks were short of the symbolic resources needed to account for and make sense of the events.

At the end of the war, there were images of the arrival of liberating armies in the camps, there were testimonials of survivors immediately following the war, and there were books prepared in homage to the victims. At that moment, however, public efforts were focused on discovering and documenting the magnitude of the crimes. During the Nuremburg trials, there was only one testimony from a survivor. These were trials in which "evidence" was primarily documentary (Wieviorka 1998, 1999).

The great shift in the significance of survivors' testimonials took place during Adolf Eichmann's trial in Jerusalem in 1961. There, the testimony of survivors played a crucial role, not only or necessarily as legal evidence but as part of an explicit strategy of those who were bringing forth the charges against Eichmann. Their objective was to bring forth onto the world stage the memory of genocide as a central part of Jewish identity. The "witness" emerged as the central feature of the trial, inaugurating what Wieviorka calls "the era of testimony," which was reproduced on an enlarged scale during the 1980s and 1990s (Wieviorka 1998).[5] The question, however, remains: Who listens? For whom are the testimonies told?

Sufficient time had to elapse, and a new generation born after the end of the war had to come of age and begin questioning their elders, in order to recognize and attempt to give meaning to the historical void that had been created in the social ability to convey and listen to testimony. As mentioned earlier, testimonial narratives could not be conveyed or interpreted at the time the events were taking place. Only with the passing of time was it possible to bear witness of testimony, which implies the social ability to listen and give meaning to the narrative of the survivors (Laub 1992a). Here we encounter one of the paradoxes of "historical trauma," which reveals the double void in the narrative: the inability or impossibility of constructing a narrative due to the dialogical void—there is no subject, and there is no audience and no listening. When dialogue becomes possible, he or she who speaks and he or she who listens begin the process of naming, of giving meaning and constructing memories. Both are needed, each is indispensable to the other, interacting in a shared space.

Along these lines, Laub points out the parallels between the listening that takes place in psychoanalytic practice and the listening in a testimonial interview. In both cases, he argues, the interactive pact or agreement is based on the nonobstructive yet visible and active presence of the person who listens. The balance is unstable and difficult to maintain, and both participants are constantly on alert. The narrative of the victim begins as an absence, as a narrative that has yet to be substantiated. Even if there are evidence and knowledge about the events, the narrative that is being produced and listened to is the location where and the process through which something new is being constructed. One could say that it is in this act that a new "truth" is being born.

Testimony includes the listener, and the listener becomes a participant, although a differentiated one, with his or her own reactions (for details and examples, see Laub 1992a). In this context, testimony in an interview becomes a process of confronting loss, of recognizing that what has been lost will never return, "only this time with the sense that you are not alone any longer—that someone can be there as your companion—knowing you, . . . someone saying: 'I'll be with you in the very process of your losing me. I am your witness'" (Laub 1992a, 91–92).

The ways in which testimony is elicited and produced have some bearing on the results that are obtained.[6] As Michael Pollak points out, judicial testimony and, to a lesser degree, testimony given to commissions engaged in historical investigation are clearly determined by the intended audience. In the case of the oral history interview, also, testimony is solicited by a third party, but such interviews take place in a negotiated space and in the context of the personal relationship between the interviewer and the informant. Finally, autobiographical writing reflects a personal decision on the part of the writer to speak publicly. Each of these as well as other modes of expression implies different degrees of spontaneity, different negotiations between the person and his or her own identity, and different instrumentalities of the speech act (Pollak 1990; Bourdieu 1985).

In all cases, there is an "alter" who is present and actively listening, although there may be varying degrees of empathy between the witness and the listener. When there is no empathy, when telling one's story—whether repetitive or not—does not include another person who is actively listening and asking, the act of telling may turn into a reactualization or repetition of the event narrated. The telling does not necessarily provide any relief but rather entails a reactualization of the trauma. "The absence of an empathic listener, or more radically, the absence of an *addressable other,* an other who can hear the anguish of one's memories and thus affirm and recognize their realness, annihilates the story. And it is, precisely, this ultimate annihilation of a narrative that, fundamentally, *cannot be heard* and of a story that *cannot be witnessed,* which constitutes the mortal eighty-first blow" (Laub 1992b, 68).

How is the ability to listen generated? The issue is not about having an "internal" audience comprised of those who share a community or comprise a collective "we." In those inward-oriented spaces, testimonial narrative can at times become ritualized repetition rather than an act of creative dialogue. What is needed are "others" with the ability to ask, to express curiosity for a painful past, as well as to have compassion and empathy. This creative construction is enabled much more by "alterity" than by identification between the speaker and the listener, and this is not easily achieved. As Semprún (1997) asks, "[c]an people hear everything, imagine everything?" (14).

Psychoanalysts specialize in this labor of listening in a therapeutic context and usually in an individualized manner. For social projects of listening and rescuing testimonies, besides the active initiative of "memory entrepreneurs," what is required are some other special qualities. What are needed are interviewers and social spaces of listening committed to "preservation" of the remnants and traces of the past embedded in life experience, but much more than that: a keen awareness of the subjective processes of the people that are invited to narrate their life experiences.

In broader social contexts, it is possible to identify some of those "others" willing to listen in the coming of age of new generations—new generations that ask questions and express a willingness to understand, but who are free of the historical burden that weighs upon the common sense of a generation or a social group that has been victimized. Other "others" may also play this role—individuals and groups that approach the issues involved bringing with them other historical frameworks and other cultural understandings. Here, as in many other social processes, intercultural dialogue is a source of creativity.

There are two additional points that are brought to the fore by reflections that have emerged in the aftermath of the Shoah. The first, which is raised by Claude Lanzmann in relation to the testimonies presented in his film *Shoah*, refers to the impossibility of understanding what has transpired. Lanzmann insists on this point. His objective is not to comprehend or understand the causes of the extermination so as to be able to elaborate a narrative to be transmitted. For the author, asking *why* the Jews were exterminated is an obscenity.[7] The experience is not recorded from the place of understanding causes and conditions, motives, and patterns of behavior. It is precisely what is not understood, what is incomprehensible, that generates the creative act of transmission (Lanzmann 1995).

This impossibility of understanding may be taken as a limit. Asking the "why" and the attempts to unravel the political, ideological, psychological, and sociocultural matrix that led to those extreme situations have been a permanent force behind research and inquiry in all arenas of knowledge. In this context, it is not a matter of obscenity but of the restlessness and anxiety for knowledge.

A second issue has to do with the relationship between testimony and "truth." When working on the relationship between testimony and trauma, the consideration of the "truth" is displaced from factual description to subjective narratives that convey the truths that reside inside the silences, fears, and ghosts that visit the narrator in his or her dreams, in smells or in repetitive sounds.[8] Here we encounter once again the dilemmas of "historical truth" and the veracity of remembrance (Portelli 1997; Ricouer 2000).[9]

The relationship between trauma and the ability to represent or narrate can be examined from another angle, the angle of discursivity. Ernst van Alphen raises the issue of the impossibility of narrating for those who have lived through the extermination of the Shoah. Is it because of the nature of the event itself, because of its extreme character? Or is it related to the restrictions and limitations of language, of the symbolic systems available at the time? He argues that the traumatic dimension of the event implies a "semiotic incapacity" when going through the event itself, and this incapacity precludes the possibility of "experiencing" and representing it in terms of the available symbolic order. For survivors, this semiotic incapacity may be rooted in their impossibility of occupying an active subject position. This may show up as an ambiguous subjectivity in which the survivor is not able to locate him or herself in either of the two subject positions available within the habitual interpretive frame—victim or perpetrator? Active subject or passive object of the actions of others? In this case, the difficulty of experiencing the event resides in the phenomenon of ambiguity and in the absence of rhetorical tools needed to handle it. Another situation is that of a total negation of subjectivity, in which survivors find themselves reduced to "nothing." They may be able to narrate the terrible events that happened to them in the camp, but they do so with distance and without emotion, as if their subjectivity itself had been destroyed in the camp (van Alphen 1999).

The difficulties are linked to the existent (or nonexistent) frameworks for narrating the Nazi extermination. They may result from the lack of a plot or a narrative model that could allow survivors to narrate events with any meaningful coherence, or from the fact that existing interpretive frameworks were not effective because they were contradicted or negated by the subjective trajectory of the survivor. This is the case with survivors who are expected to narrate their biography using a linear structure, with a normal "before," a rupture as a result of his or her life through the extermination in the camp, and an "after" marking a phase of reconstruction (van Alphen 1999; 1997, chapter 2).[10]

With this discursive foundation, and dependent on the narrative frameworks existent in a particular culture, the issue of testimony returns to an arena where the individual and the collective meet. Even individual memory, implying an interaction between the past and the present, is culturally and collectively framed. Memory is not an object that is simply there to be extracted, but rather it is produced by active subjects that share a culture and an *ethos*.

The Testimony of the Voiceless

There is another source of interest and debate regarding testimony. It comes from the area of Latin Americanist North American cultural studies. During the past decade, there has been an explosion of critical writings about testimony and its relationship to literature. In general, these testimonial texts are based on the collaboration between the person who is going to give his or her testimony—who tends to be a member of a socially dispossessed group (or of the "Third World") or some other subaltern category—and a privileged mediator, who typically comes from a different cultural background, usually from the "Center" and/or the higher strata of society. From the perspective of the "good consciousness" of the mediator, the aim of the text is to make visible to the world something that until then had been invisible and silenced by the powerful.[11] These texts also seek to raise consciousness and denounce situations of exploitation (Gugelberger 1996b).

The seductive potential of this genre is notorious indeed. Inviting the reader to participate and witness the emergence of a subject and a voice inspires complicity and nurtures a feeling of intimacy between the narrator and the reader that, at least on the surface, is couched in notions of authenticity (Sommer 1991, 32). In her analysis of Rigoberta Menchú's testimonial, Doris Sommer reveals some of the rhetorical mechanisms of the text, by which in fact Menchú maintains control over the social distance between herself and her audience. One of these is the cultural affirmation of her right to keep silent (as she states it, "Indians have been very careful not to disclose any details of their communities"; quoted by Sommer 1991, 33). Her ability to elicit the curiosity of the reader comes from her performativity (Sommer 1991, 35).

What is most important for our purposes in Sommer's analysis is the movement between identification and distance that is established between Menchú and her readers. Throughout the text, Menchú calls attention to the distance between her and "the others." This is a departure from the usual manner in which first-person autobiographical narratives are constructed. These writings are expected to be revealing, intimate, and almost confessional. Yet as she refers to her "secrets," Menchú is constantly excluding the reader from her intimate circle, highlighting difference repeatedly. There is no place for identification here, but there is a place for dialogue.

On the other hand, and in clear contrast with autobiographical writing, Menchú presents herself as the voice of a collectivity, as if her testimonial had a "plural subject." The testimonial of Bolivian Domitila Barrios has a similar structure (Viezzer 1977). The use of the first person, the "I," does not elicit identification. The singular represents the plural but in a way that excludes the reader. This is the case of an *ore*, not a *ñande*. Sommer (1991) writes:

> In rhetorical terms, whose political consequences should be evident in what follows, there is a fundamental difference here between the *metaphor* of autobiography and heroic narrative in general, which assumes an identity-by-substituting one (superior) signifier for another (I for we, leader for follower, Christ for the faithful), and metonymy, a lateral move of identification-through-relationship, which acknowledges the possible differences among "us" as components of a centerless whole. This is where we can come in as readers, invited to be *(estar)* with the speaker rather than to be *(ser)* her. (39)

The case of Rigoberta Menchú is a good illustration of the effects that a testimonial can have on different audiences, as well as of their transformations over time. Both the book and the figure of Menchú were venerated and practically canonized, especially within progressive academic circles in the United States. Her 1992 Nobel Peace Prize made her a world-famous figure. It thrust her into an international political arena that required the elaboration of appropriate tactics and strategies and created both allies and enemies in diverse quarters. In the late 1990s, her testimony once again entered the spotlight, in the aftermath of David Stoll's book (1999) casting doubt on the veracity of the information that it contained.

We need not enter into the details of the controversy generated in the arena of cultural studies in the United States by Stoll's claims (see Arias 2001), since they are beyond the scope and objective of this discussion. Yet the episode raises two pertinent issues. The first concerns the nature of "historical truth." There is little doubt that Menchú's text contains descriptions of events that are presented in the first person but that were not directly witnessed by Menchú herself. Does this fact invalidate her testimony? What level of truth is being demanded of her? Is it factual or symbolic? Where does the boundary between "reality" and "fiction" lie? Are not processes of social construction always involved? All of these questions clearly indicate that no text can be interpreted outside the context in which it is produced and received, including the political dimensions of the phenomenon.

Second, it is also evident that the testimonial character of Menchú's narrative is not based on her personal presence as a direct witness of all the events she describes therein. This is the position that she herself has defended. The narrative is based on a collective presence, which requires that the text, written in the first person, be read as a synthetic expression of collective experiences. This stance ultimately depends on the argument made in previous chapters regarding the political inexpediency of the distinction between "direct protagonists" and "others." Furthermore, these distances and dissonances between the events as they took place and the narrative once again call for a deeper critical examination of them in order to better understand the relationship between events and representations.

In fact, the reference to the debate about testimonial texts and literature is presented here insofar as it allows for discerning several key issues. First is the recognition of the mediating role of the editor of the text, which reinforces the notion that dialogue is a constitutive element of testimonial narratives. This dialogic mediation is analogous to the listener-audience in the construction of survivors' testimony. Second, a distinction is drawn between the individualized autobiography and a testimonial with a plural subject, an "I" that is representative of a particular social condition and particular social struggles.[12] Third, although the narrative establishes the author's complicity with the reader, the text invites dialogue (which Sommer would call horizontal rather than hierarchical, as would be the case with autobiography) rather than identification. Finally, the control and manipulation of silences and of what is not said are key rhetorical instruments for marking these differences and for clearly establishing the "alterity" of the reader.

This kind of testimonial text makes explicit the range of rhetorical forms that a personal narrative can take. At one extreme, the act of narration is motivated by willpower and by the rationality behind the elaboration of a public political strategy. In such a case, mediation is in a sense instrumental for reaching a broad audience with messages that can be interpreted according to preexisting cultural frameworks (and which the narrating subject does not necessarily know in-depth). At the other extreme, we have traumatized subjects who are able to construct a narrative—sometimes without a full appropriation of meaning—based on the intervention of others who strive to create a personalized and active space of dialogue and listening.

Obviously, reality is not so starkly polarized, and circulation and dialogue can take very diverse forms that combine strategies of enunciation and diverse modalities for the expression of subjectivity.

Testimonials of Repression in the Southern Cone

In the opening pages of *Mi habitación, mi celda* (My room, my cell) (Celiberti and Garrido 1989), Lilian Celiberti narrates the details of her kidnapping (together with her two children) in Porto Alegre, Brazil, and their clandestine transfer to Uruguay. This was the beginning of a prison ordeal that lasted five long years until her release in 1983. The narrative of her detention suggests that as an unabashed political activist, she was aware of the risks she was taking and of the potential consequences these could have. Even at a time when little was publicly known about Operation Condor,[13] her narrative suggests that she was conscious of the dangers involved in her activities and about the various measures she needed to take to protect her safety. In other words, although it was unexpected, her detention was well within the realm of the possible. What was probably not imaginable, however, was that her kidnapping would compromise the lives of her children.

In the pages that follow, Celiberti describes the strategies she developed to try to prevent her transfer from Brazil to Uruguay. With the anguish of someone whose life is in danger, but who also feels responsible for the fate of her children, she begins to "invent" ways to veer off the route that her captors had planned. All her actions—her successful attempts to convince them when reaching the border that they needed to return to Porto Alegre, her unsuccessful attempt to publicize her kidnapping to the Brazilian press and military authorities—appear to come from a sharp, creative, and active mind, acting and strategizing at full speed. Despite the detailed description of her actions and strategies, however, Celiberti speaks of the situation as an event "without words." Yet the narrative does not appear to be lacking words. Is her

reflection about this absence of words a retrospective "normalization" of the event? Or is it a way to refer to the silence that shrouds
her memory in the present (Dove 2000)?

This autobiographical narrative of a political activist who tells
her story of detention is quite different from many testimonies, particularly those of the mothers of the detained-disappeared, who lived
through the violent detention and disappearances of their children as
completely unexpected and inexplicable events. In Celiberti's case, there
is no rupture or lapse at that moment. This would come later on, during her time in solitary confinement in the Uruguayan jail. At the time
of her detention, the fracture and the void show up forcefully in relation to her children. "I have lived again many times the moment I said
good-by to Camilo and Francesca. I cannot think about it without me
dying a little . . ." (Celiberti and Garrido 1989, 21). In the case of the
mothers of the disappeared who lived through the events as unexpected, the "catastrophe" is massive and total; existing interpretive frames
do not allow making sense of what is taking place. Soon, however,
the reasonable explanations—such as thinking that the missing relative was picked up "by mistake"—fall by the wayside. Bewilderment,
disbelief, and uncertainty set in when the answer to the search for a
disappeared person in one police station after another or the request
of help from "influential" friends is an absence, a void, or the actual
negation of the disappeared person's very existence.

The traumatic path implies a break in the ability to live through an
"experience" that makes sense and has some meaning. There is a sus-
pension of temporality, expressed in the repetitions, reappearances, and
recurrent specters that follow. The possibility of giving testimony—in
the dual sense of the notion of witness presented earlier—requires a
time for subjective reconstruction and for distancing past and present.
This process involves the elaboration and construction of a memory of
the lived past but not a total immersion in that past. "I return," says
Celiberti, "but not entirely" (21). A part of the past must remain there,
buried, in order to be able to symbolize it in the present without identifying with the past, which would lead to a permanent reliving of it.

In sum, there are two links involved in testimonials, links that
simultaneously create and erase distance. Both, I believe, are necessary
for the (re)construction of personal identity and selfhood. The first is a
relationship with an "other" who can help, through a dialogue based
on alterity, to construct a meaningful social narrative.[14] Practically
every testimonial has this dialogic quality, which involves someone

who asks the questions and edits and "normalizes" the narrative. This alterity is then transferred to the relationship with the reader. What is elicited is not identification but recognition of difference.

Second, the relationship to the past is one of both proximity and distance—returning to the extreme situation, as well as returning *from* it. Without this second possibility, which implies coming back and taking distance, testimony becomes impossible. Enunciating the experience of death, as both Semprún and Celiberti do, does not require reliving it, but rather the ability of incorporating it into life in the present and the future. Locating memory in the present gives that memory a fundamental quality that enables survivors to access and construct that past without fully returning to its horrors.

A large number of testimonies of survivors of illegal detention camps and prisons, as well as of their relatives—mothers, children, and spouses—have seen the light in the 1990s in the Southern Cone. Initiatives include autobiographical books, documentary movies, television interviews, and oral history archives. These are not only market-driven phenomena (what critics refer to as "the boom of the biography and the testimonial"); they respond also to complex searches for personal meanings and for the reconstruction of social networks. Many of these projects are driven by political and educational concerns—to transmit the memories of collective experiences of political struggles, as well as the horrors of repression, in an attempt to imagine desirable futures and to forcefully underline the notion of "never again."

The testimonial turn includes other more troublesome and ambiguous facets: how are the confessions and testimonies of repressors be interpreted? What about the writings of those who, after being abducted, became collaborators of the military regimes? Cultural critiques in the region have made important contributions to the analysis and interpretation of these texts, showing the ambiguities and *gray zones* that they embody. Nelly Richard's analysis of the autobiographies of two Chilean women who became "traitors" and after transition gave testimony incriminating repressors shows the intricacies of their attempt to regain their place in society and is a model of this type of critique (Richard 1998; also Franco 2002, chapter 10).

In Synthesis

The testimonial, as a construction of memories, implies a multiplicity of voices and the circulation of multiple "truths" and silences—as in Marta Diana's book (1996), where the women who are interviewed never speak of their active participation in armed struggle. The silences, what is not said, may be expressions of traumatic lapses. Yet they may also be, as in the case of Rigoberta Menchú and her "cultural" silences, strategies to establish social distance with the reader, and more broadly, with the "other." These silences can also be responses to what those others are prepared to hear (Pollak and Heinich 1986), or attempts to reestablish human dignity and a sense of "shame" as a way to reconstitute spaces of intimacy that do not necessarily have to be exposed to the gaze of others.

By bringing into play a horror that has not been worked through subjectively, pain and its physical marks may impede the construction of testimonial narrative. Traumatic suffering may deprive the victim of the recourse to language, and so prevent testimonial enunciation, or it may allow for narrations that are devoid of subjectivity. On the other hand, the "others," those who listen, may also find limits in their ability to comprehend that which is embodied in the corporal and subjective space of the sufferer. Traumatic traces, often silenced to avoid the suffering of the person who bears them, may at times be denied or not heard by others due either to a political decision or to the lack of a social network ready or willing to incorporate them. All that exists is a vacuum, a space in which silence lingers and immobilizes the expression and circulation of testimonial narrative. This can lead both to the glorification and the stigmatization of the victims, as the only people whose claims are either endorsed or rejected. In either of these cases, the dissociation between the victims and the rest of society is deepened.

Through personal testimony, those who suffered directly begin to speak and narrate their experiences and their suffering. These testimonials are at the same time essential sources of information about what happened during the repressive regimes, an exercise in personal and social memory insofar as they are narratives that attempt to make some sense of the past, and a medium of creative personal expression for both the narrator and for those who ask the questions or listen.

Two further points are pertinent here. The first is that although the possibility of narration may be seen initially as breaking through silence and traumatic lapses, this is not always the case. Even when survivors are able to respond to interviewers' questions or to construct a narrative, the difficulties and obstacles they face may be enormous. These difficulties reflect the discrepancies between the events lived through and the lack of narrative frameworks through which to express them.[15]

Some testimonies are devoid of subjectivity; others seem to be ritualized repetitions of a narrative of suffering (van Alphen 1999). In turn, the listener may feel alienated or detached from the narratives. Furthermore, the willingness and openness for listening vary over time: there seem to be moments or periods in history when the capacity to listen and understand arises, and others when listening is simply not possible. There are also moments in which the social, institutional, and political climate is favorable for the production of such narratives, and others when a feeling of saturation and excess prevails. Once again, this implies the need of historicizing testimony, thus urging to take into consideration the temporality and historicity of personalized narratives and of the possibilities of listening.

Second, a word of caution regarding the inherent "goodness" of testimonials and the interpretive frame used to assign them meaning is necessary. The prevailing model or framework is a psychological one, which takes as its point of departure the catastrophe that brings about suffering and trauma, followed by a process of mourning, and coming to a close in a process of healing that implies the acceptance of loss. Within this individual and interpersonal process, speaking and telling have their place, which may often be cathartic or therapeutic. In current times, when the mass media are bent on making private lives public through talk shows and reality shows that flatten sentiments and intimacy by making them banal, the testimonial genre runs the risk of being turned into a banal and overexposed spectacle of horror. State terrorism and repression violated human bodies and intimacy; the reconstruction of identity after such turmoil requires that private and intimate spaces also be rebuilt. In this context, the testimonial "fads" (often modeled by the mass media) pose dangers that should not be ignored.

On the other hand, the individual or personal significance of speaking and finding a space of listening should not replace, occlude, or omit other arenas in which the labors of memory operate. This testimonial wave should not replace the urgent need for political, institutional, and juridical responses to past conflicts, nor should it overshadow symbolic, moral, or ethical ones.

Six

Engendered Memories

If we close our eyes and attempt to envision the "human" side of the dictatorships in the Southern Cone, one image dominates the scene: the Madres de Plaza de Mayo. Then, other women come into sight: the *Familiares, Abuelas, Viudas, Comadres* (Relatives, Grandmothers, Widows, and Other Kin) of the disappeared or of political prisoners, denouncing the arrests and searching for their children (which in the image are usually sons), their grandchildren, their husbands, or partners. On the other side, we see the military in full display of their masculinity. There is a second image that emerges, specific to the Argentine case: that of young pregnant female prisoners, giving birth in clandestine detention centers and then disappearing. This image is haunted by the uncertainty about the whereabouts of their children, kidnapped or stolen, who would later be given false identities. On the other side, once again, is the image of the hypermasculine military.

The gender contrast in these images is clear and comes back time and again in a wide range of contexts. Personalized symbols of pain and suffering tend to become embodied in women, while institutional repressive mechanisms appear to "belong" to men.

In the television reporting linked to the Pinochet case, from the time of his arrest in London in October 1998 and all through his detention in Chile up to 2001, the differential presence of men and women was also noteworthy. It was women who ran the human rights organizations demanding justice; they were also the most visible presence in street demonstrations celebrating and supporting the general's arrest. But it was also women who were the most arduous and emotional defenders of Pinochet's historical legacy. And it is men who, on all three sides of the case (the accusers, the defendants, the judges), dominate the institutional aspects of the matter.

Is there anything more to say about gender and repression? Or about gender and memory? The attempt to engage these issues is based on the belief that, as in many other areas of research, unless there is a conscious and focused effort to elaborate analytical questions from a gender perspective, the end result is likely to be a stereotypical image in which the women suffer and the military men dominate; alternatively, gender may be rendered invisible once again.

Repression Is Gendered

The repression carried out by the dictatorships of the Southern Cone had clear gender specificities.[1] It affected men and women differently, given their differential positions within the gender system—positions that imply different life experiences and markedly different hierarchically organized social relations.[2]

Let us begin by examining the physical or bodily experience of repression, involving actual practices and direct victims of torture, prison, disappearance, execution, and exile. There are intercountry variations as well as changes over time in each country with respect to the prevailing type of repression. There are also differences in the demographic characteristics of the victims. There were more men than women among the executed and the disappeared, a difference that seems to have been more marked in Chile than in Argentina or in Uruguay. The proportion of young people among the victims was higher in the latter two countries. One should remember here that the 1973 military coup in Chile was directed against a governing socialist administration. Repression, in this case, was concentrated against politicians and government employees, thus making the proportion of adult males higher among the total victims. In Argentina, Uruguay, and Brazil, the most violent repression was directed against militant groups (including armed guerrilla movements), in which there were higher proportions of young people. The sexual division of labor in these countries implies a higher proportion of men than of women in "public" roles, including government positions, and in political and labor union activism (this was much more so in the 1960s and 1970s than it is today). The proportion of men to women was less skewed in student movements and armed guerrilla movements, where during that time women already had a significant presence.

In acts of direct repression, power is also exercised in the framework of gender relations. The dominant gender system identifies masculinity with domination and aggression, and these characteristics are heightened in military identity. Femininity is conceived as an ambivalent condition, combining the spiritual superiority of women (even the very notions of "nation" and "motherland" are feminized) with submissiveness and passivity in the face of the desires and orders of men. Rituals of power in the public sphere (military salutes, parades, and so on) have a performative quality, through which they unambiguously stage the opposition between the active/empowered masculine subject and the passive/excluded feminized audience, an audience that may at times involve the entire civilian population.[3]

Masculine military power in the public sphere—with its rituals and repetitive practices of representation involving uniforms, parades, weaponry, and so on—is accompanied by performances materialized in and through bodies and concrete practices in specific spaces, particularly in the places of torture. There, the masculinity of the torturers reaffirmed itself in its absolute power to produce pain and suffering. Torture was part of a "ceremony of initiation" in the detention camps, during which a person was deprived of all access to his or her identity: clothing, personal belongings, and sight (it was common for prisoners to be blindfolded at all times). "Humanity itself is suspended. . . . the blindfold and the loss of vision intensify the insecurity and disorientation. . . . Torturers do not see the face of their victims. They punish bodies without faces. They punish subversives, not men" (Calveiro 1998, 62). The use of animal nicknames, such as Tiger, Jaguar, and Puma, and the initiation ceremonies of new torturers are "moments of exaltation, when the torturer felt as if he were God," with the power to turn another being into a passive victim, into a body to be penetrated (Franco 1992, esp. 107).[4] Direct repression against women was related to their role as active militants. Yet women were also kidnapped and tortured by state agents as a result of their familial identities and specifically their ties to men—partners, husbands in particular, but sons as well—with the purpose extracting information about the political activities of these relatives.[5] The identification of womanhood with motherhood and the family cast women in a particular role, namely that of being blamed for the "bad ways" and deviations of their children and other relatives (Filc 1997).

All existing reports about torture indicate that the female body was always a "special" object for torturers. The treatment of women always included a high degree of sexual violence. Women's bodies— their vagina, uterus, and breasts—linked to women's identities as sexual objects, as wives and as mothers, were clear objects of sexual torture (Bunster 1991; Taylor 1997). We must also remember that many of the imprisoned women were young and attractive and thus more vulnerable to sexual harassment and violence.

For men, imprisonment and torture were acts of "feminization," in which they were transformed into passive, impotent, and dependent beings. Sexual violence was part of torture, and genitals became an unvarying point of reference—the mark of circumcision among Jewish victims became the justification for increased exposure to torture, and the references to penis size and the application of electricity to the testicles became regular practices. All these were ways of transforming men into inferior beings and, in the very act, establishing military "virility."[6] Men were forced "to live like women," becoming keenly aware of their bodily necessities: to be like a woman or to die like a man (Franco 1992; for a testimony, see Tavares 1999).

The duality opposing the masculine and active on the one hand and the feminine and passive on the other was seen as natural among the military. This was also the dominant interpretive framework among guerrilla groups and in society at large. In the representations of the *guerrillera* (the female guerrilla fighter) that circulated in the Argentine media during dictatorship, femininity was always ambiguous. On one hand the image was one of a masculinized woman, in uniform and bearing arms, rejecting femininity altogether. The media also recognized, however, the women militants who acted as young innocent girls using their youth and femininity to deceive and infiltrate in order to carry out attacks.[7] As a mirror image, the guerrilla movement also had difficulties in incorporating the femininity of women militants. The acceptance of women was always in doubt, and when they demonstrated their abilities in armed operations, they were seen as "pseudomales" (Franco 1992, 108). A desexualized and masculinized self-identification is also evident in several testimonials written by female ex-prisoners and former militants.

Given the gender system prevalent in family relations, besides becoming many of the direct victims of repression, women were predominantly and essentially "indirect" victims. This is the role with which they are most commonly associated—as relatives of victims: mothers, grandmothers, and to a lesser extent, wives, sisters, daughters, and girlfriends. When kidnapping men, the repressive system affected women in their family and kinship roles, that is, in the core of their traditional identities as mothers and wives. From these social locations, and as a way to survive and meet their expected "familial obligations," women had to mobilize other kinds of energy, those based on their "traditional" roles within the family, anchored in feelings, love, and an ethic of caring and nurturing—a logic that is quite distant from the realm of the political.

Two "typically feminine" kinds of response emerged in this context: in the public sphere, the creation and participation in human rights organizations based on direct kinship with the victims; and in the private sphere, the struggle for family subsistence and the adjustments and changes precipitated by the new circumstances. It is not by simple coincidence or chance that human rights organizations have had familial identifications (Mothers, Grandmothers, Children, Widows, or Other Kin). It is also not by chance that the leaders and members of these organizations were primarily female. Their gendered character is also evident in some of the symbols and rituals employed by these groups—the use of scarves and diapers, photographs and flowers.

On the private family side, women in these circumstances also had to take responsibility for the economic subsistence of their families when the men were kidnapped or imprisoned. Many women became the main providers for their households. Based on both their feelings and the sense of family responsibility, these women were forced to mobilize their personal resources to care for and feed their families and others, be it in their own domestic households or, at times, in communal initiatives such as soup kitchens and small cooperative endeavors.

In "normal" times, many women have to confront domesticity and the responsibilities involved in kinship and parenting by themselves, alone. This happens in diverse social contexts and personal circumstances (divorces, abandonment) and may often be linked to poverty. Yet the circumstances of the women who had to take up these responsibilities as a result of the arrest, kidnapping, or disappearance of their partners are intrinsically different, for themselves and for their children and other relatives. In the first place, the climate of terror in which they lived often required silencing what had happened, and even covering up personal suffering. To avoid arousing suspicion, women had to attempt to maintain a semblance of normal life for their children, "as if nothing had happened." Fear and silence were constantly present, and they exacted a very high emotional cost. In many cases, solitude was a central feature of the experience. Whether because they did not want to put at risk other relatives or friends, or because those relatives or friends distanced themselves due to fear or disapproval, the social networks within which everyday domestic life used to take place were completely destroyed, fractured, broken.[8]

Exile is a different story. It was often the result of the political commitment of men, and women had to accompany their partners or relatives not as a result of their own political project and activism but as wives, daughters, or mothers. Under such circumstances, the effects of the experience of exile are undoubtedly different from an exile resulting from one's own political project or public commitment. As with other circumstances of repression, the gendered character of exile is an issue about which little has been done in a systematic or analytical form, beyond the accumulation of testimonies.

We must not forget, however, that men too were "indirect" victims, and as such they are completely invisible. Little is known about this particular personal experience. It has not been a massive one to be sure—there were few husbands or male relatives of female activists and militants that did not themselves engage in public political activity. Furthermore, such family arrangements tend to be socially invisible, in part because they go against "normal" social patterns and expectations. Existing testimonies, such as that of Emilio Mignone (1991) regarding the kidnapping and disappearance of his daughter, have been published by public figures and tend to focus more on the public and proactive dimensions of the event, with little or no mention of the private or domestic side of it.

Military regimes resulted in significant transformations in the daily activities of both men and women. Fear and uncertainty permeated social spaces and practices, particularly in public spaces outside family relations. Since men tend to be more active within such spaces, perhaps they felt a greater impact. Citing the Chilean case, José Olavarría points to four public spaces that were disarticulated by the "new order": the workplace, political parties, labor unions, and "nightlife." Until the

1970s, these spaces had played significant roles in the everyday experience of masculinity, insofar as they represented instances of "homosociality, of exchanges between men, that at the same time linked and enabled constant flows between different sectors of Chilean society" (Olavarría 2001, 4). The transformations of these spaces wrought by the repression unleashed by the dictatorship had the effects of limiting the range of networks and social relations, "in the case of men, to the sphere of the family, the neighborhood, and work itself" (5). This was not a case of imprisonment or torture but one of feelings of passivity and impotence.

Repression was carried out by masculine and patriarchal institutions—the armed forces and the police. These institutions imagined themselves as missionaries destined to reestablish the "natural" (gender) order of things. In their visions, they had to permanently remind women of their place in society—as the guardians of the social order, as the nurturers of husbands and children, and in charge of protecting family harmony and tranquility. It was they who were at fault for the transgressions of their children, and also for the subversion of the "natural" hierarchy between men and women. The military regimes supported and tried to impose a discourse and an ideology based on family values. The patriarchal family was more than the central metaphor of their regimes. It was literal reality (Filc 1997).[9]

A Different Level: Men and Women Remember . . .

Both direct experience and intuition suggest that women and men develop different abilities to remember. Insofar as gender socialization implies paying more attention to certain social and cultural arenas than to others, and personal identities tend to be defined in relation to gender roles in work or family, it is to be expected that there will be a certain gender correlation with practices of recollection and narrative memory.[10] There is some qualitative evidence that suggests that women tend to remember events in greater detail, while men tend to generate more synthetic narratives. Other evidence suggests that women more often express feelings, while men convey their recollections within logical and rational frameworks, and also that women more commonly refer to their intimate sphere and interpersonal relationships, whether within the family or within political activism. Women tend to remember everyday life, the economic situation of their families, what they were supposed to be doing at every minute of the day, what was happening in their neighborhoods and communities, their fears and feelings of insecurity. They remember within the framework of family relationships, because women's subjective experience of time is organized by and linked to reproductive events and affective ties (Leydesdorff, Passerini, and Thompson 1996).

In the case of memories of repression, moreover, many women narrate their memories in the context of their more traditional gender role, that of caregiver and nurturer, of "living for others." This is linked to the definition of an identity centered on tending to and caring for others, generally within the frame of family relations. The ambiguity of the position, between that of active agent and that of passive companion and caretaker, may show up then in a displacement of their own identity, prompting them to "narrate the other." In the double sense of the notion of witness that was presented earlier, this implies the choice to be a witness-observer of another person's protagonism (a disappeared son, for example), negating or silencing testimony about her own life experiences, although they will undoubtedly slip into the narratives that are apparently centered on others.

Men's memories, and their modes of narration, point in another direction. Their testimonies are often found in public documents, judicial testimonies, and journalistic reports. Spoken narratives, narrated in public contexts and transcribed into "material evidence," are framed within expectations of justice and political change. While these testimonies may undoubtedly empower and legitimize the voice of the victim in these contexts, their "testimonial" function is centered in the factual description, narrated as precisely as possible, about the materiality of torture and political violence. The less emotion and subjective involvement in the narrative the better, because oral testimony in these contexts is meant to replace the "material traces" of the crime.

In fact, what is implicit in the preceding paragraph is an initial differentiation between different social frameworks for the expression of memories, and in a next stage the question about gender differences within each of them can arise. Court testimony, be it from men or women, follows a preestablished format that is tied to the notion of factual, cold, and precise juridical evidence. This kind of public testimony is different than others, such as those in historical archives, those elicited by researchers, the testimonial texts written by survivors, witnesses, and victims, and literary "representations," which are necessarily distanced from past events (Taylor 1997, chapter 6; Pollak and Heinich 1986).[11]

Men and women develop different ways of expressing their memories publicly. This issue has been studied in the case of Shoah survivors. The best-known testimonial narratives are those of men—the great writers like Primo Levi, Jean Amery, and Jorge Semprún. As Glanz (2001) points out, women wrote less, but there were also fewer women survivors because their ability to be the "carriers of life" made them particularly dangerous to their captors. "To eliminate a race," argues Glanz, "the women had to be eliminated" (123).[12] But of course there were women who survived and who, out of personal or political necessity or through the mediation of third parties, narrated their stories and their memories.

In the concentration camps, men and women were kept separate; thus testimonial narratives render different spheres and experiences. Women's narratives emphasize their vulnerability as sexual beings and the affective and nurturing bonds that developed among them. In these narratives, physical and social survival is linked to reproduction and the re-creation of the roles learned through their gender socialization— an emphasis on cleanliness, on their abilities to sew and mend clothing that allowed them to keep up their physical appearance, on the care of others, and on life in communal spaces within the camps that allowed them to reinvent their family-based bonds (Goldenberg 1990). In fact, some of the evidence provided by the survivors of Nazi concentration camps suggests that women "fared better" than men in the face of attempts to destroy their personal integrity because their ego investments were not so focused on themselves but directed toward their surroundings and those around them.

The demographic reality in the case of the dictatorships in the Southern Cone was markedly different. Women can narrate the experiences of others, their own experiences as direct victims (survivors of repression in its diverse forms) or as "indirect" victims, and their activities as militants in the human rights movement. A significant number of autobiographical texts and interview-based testimonial renderings of experiences of repression in the region have been produced. What are lacking are systematic comparative studies of the testimonies of male and female survivors and witnesses that take a gender perspective (but see Franco 1992 and 2002).

One way to think about gender and memory derives from what has become by now a traditional approach within both feminist inquiry and current reflection on the testimonial genre (Gugelberger 1996a): "making visible the invisible," "giving voice to those that have no voice." Women's voices tell different stories than men's, thus introducing into the public space of debate a plurality of viewpoints and worldviews. This perspective also implies the recognition and legitimization of experiences other than those considered dominant or hegemonic (mostly those of men and those enunciated from positions of power). This fosters the circulation of diverse narratives: those that focus on political militancy, on suffering related to repression, on the organization of everyday life under repressive regimes, or on emotions and subjectivity. These are the "other" faces of history and memory, the untold beginning to be voiced and listened to.

Let us take the case of the (mostly Korean) women that were kidnapped by the Japanese armed forces to establish "comfort stations," a type of sexual slavery designed to serve the Japanese occupation forces during World War II (Chizuko 1999). It is estimated that anywhere between 80,000 and 120,000 women were forced into these camps. Although the existence of these comfort stations was widely known both in Korea and Japan (a book was published on the subject in the 1970s, and it became a best-seller in Japan), the sexual slavery to which these women were subject was redefined as a crime only in the 1980s and became a highly controversial and visible political issue only in the 1990s.[13]

The women who were kidnapped in Korea remained silent for fifty years. There was not a single testimony until the early 1990s, and it is quite likely that there are still many victims who have not come forth.[14] They began to speak, in part, as the result of the efforts of the feminist movement, particularly through the creation of a Korean women's organization that encouraged the victims to tell their stories. For these women, narrating their testimonies offered the opportunity to recuperate a silenced past and in the process begin to regain their human dignity.

But there is more to this story. In this coming to voice of the victims, so argues Chizuko, history itself is remade. Whereas before the debate about "what actually happened" was maintained within the bounds of a history written "from above,"[15] when a victim (or survivor) "begins spinning the fragmentary thread of her own narrative, telling a story that announces 'my reality was not the kind of thing you think,' an alternative history emerges, relativizing the dominant one at a stroke" (Chizuko 1999, 143). We know, however, that testimonial narratives are constructed in the interaction of the interview situation, and the power relation with the interviewer (be it in court, talking to a journalist, or in the context of a feminist support network) leads the subject to accommodate the narrative to what is expected. In this manner, a repetitive and stylized model of victim was constructed, and the vast diversity of situations and narratives remains invisible or is occluded.

In this case, the process of giving voice to the muted and the speechless is part of the transformation of the meanings of the past, involving profound redefinitions and rewriting of history. Its function goes far beyond enriching and complementing the dominant voices that establish the framework of public memory. Without setting out to do so, these voices defied the framework within which history was being written, by challenging the models through which the past was being interpreted.

Without reaching such extremes, the critique of dominant frameworks that is present in such new voices may eventually lead to a transformation of the contents and frameworks of social memory (Leydesdorff, Passerini, and Thompson 1996). This will happen to the extent that they provoke a redefinition of the notion of the public sphere itself, rather than the introduction of subordinate voices into a previously defined public sphere.

Let us consider a case that is linked to the dictatorships of the Southern Cone, the memories of torture.[16] There is little doubt that narratives of torture and the emotions they express are different in women and in men. Jean Franco (1992) points out that the personal narratives of torture victims tend to be laconic and euphemistic. Women feel shame when they narrate their experiences. In accusatory testimonials (before human rights commissions or as witnesses in trials), for example, they recount being raped without giving details or describing the event itself. In less "normalized" or bureaucratic contexts, the contrast between men and women's narratives may be sharper. Franco illustrates the difference between the story of a man who describes his experience as a "loss of his manhood" and of being "forced to live like a woman" (Valdés 1996), and the narrative of a woman who draws the strength to survive from her identity in motherhood, which allows her to keep a sense of herself during torture and feel close to other women prisoners. In this case, the testimony even mentions the ways in which, in order to "remake" the world that the torturers were seeking to destroy, she takes refuge in the children's songs that she used to sing to her daughter (Partnoy 1988).

Personal memories of prison and torture are powerfully inflected by the centrality of the body. The possibility of incorporating them into the field of social memories poses an ethical dilemma and a real paradox: the act of repression violated privacy and intimacy, breaching the cultural division between public and private arenas. Overcoming the traumatic void created by repression calls for opening up the possibility of elaborating a narrative memory of the lived events (thus turning them into an "experience" with meaning), a process that is necessarily public, in the sense that it has to be shared with others—others who will, at least in principle, be able to understand and nurture the victim. Yet despite the fact that these others are not anonymous or that they are not the perpetrators, they remain "others"—an alterity. At the same time, the recuperation of "normalcy in life" requires the reconstruction of the self, which includes the reconstruction of intimacy and privacy. At this point, silences are fundamental in these personal narratives. Often these are not lapses, but personal decisions to omit details as a way of "managing and controlling the reconstruction of identity" (Pollak and Heinich 1986, 5), tied to the "recuperation of shame" (Amati Sas 1991). How then to combine the need to construct a public narrative that at the same time contributes to the recuperation of intimacy and privacy? The paradox is real. Recognizing it may contribute to better understanding of the crucial position of the listener, attentive yet open to the differentiated contexts and needs of the person who is exposing his or herself.

Here we encounter an ethical dilemma in relation to some types of social narrative memories. Often, reading or listening to testimonies may be experienced by the reader/listener as voyeurism, as an invasion of the privacy of the he or she who is narrating. This issue takes on public importance in the debates over confidentially clauses and the motions to restrict access to the archives of repression, which include numerous documents and even personal objects (da Silva Catela 2002).

Memory and the Gender System

Finally, we must examine the effects of repression and the military regimes on the gender system itself. The reinforcement of a specific kind of family-based morality—a totalizing and totalitarian definition of normality and deviance—cannot but have significant effects. Periods of transition out of dictatorships tend to coincide—not by chance—with moments of sexual liberation, characterized by movements for the liberation of women and sexual minorities that have long been subject to repressive practices.

The issue is complex and multilayered. Women occupied active positions of leadership both in armed guerrilla groups and in the resistance to dictatorships, although in many cases these roles required women to undergo a process of masculinization in order to find legitimacy. This process was also seen in the repressive practices that the regimes used against kidnapped women. Women also had an active presence in the human rights movement. Women (mothers, relatives, grandmothers, widows, and so on) irrupted in the public arena as the bearers of the social memory of human rights violations. Their performativity and their symbolic roles also carry a strong ethical dimension, pushing to expand the limits of political negotiation by "demanding the impossible." Their social location is anchored in naturalized familial ties, and by legitimating the public expression of pain and grief, they reproduce and reinforce stereotypes and traditional roles. Finally, women have acquired a central role in the public expression of memories, as narrators, mediators, and analysts, being involved in the various genres and forms through which these memories are publicly expressed.[17]

One final comment is in order. Transformations in the gender system are very slow and difficult. To the extent that they take place, they can imply a resignification and transformation of the memories of armed struggle and of political violence and repression. In fact, the struggles over memory are traversed by existing gender relations and by the ways in which the actors of the past are visualized in terms of the stereotypes of masculinity and femininity. The challenge for the present and the future lies in critically deconstructing and analyzing the actual experiences of men and women and the existing gender images, to be able to place them in their historical context and extract from it alternatives for future change.

Seven

Transmissions, Legacies, Lessons

Let me begin with some cases and images.

Immediately following the end of World War II, some Jewish survivors were able to maintain (or recuperate) their private cultural lives, in which Yiddish occupied a central place. Their collective culture, however, was lost. "The massacre was not simply the destruction of a given community, the death of a specific person. It was the total abolition of a collectivity, a culture, a way of life, of that called *yiddishkeit*" (Wieviorka 1998, 46). In this context, the *transmission* of ways of being and lifestyles to the new generations became extremely difficult, if not impossible. Survivors felt the urgency of rescuing their dead from the hands of oblivion. This sparked an obsession with the production of *Yizker-bikher* (books of memory) characterized by long lists of names and photographs of the dead. Yet while transmission was the main impetus behind them, these books were ignored and forgotten by the children of those who authored them. The bond across generations had been fractured by the death of the grandparents. And when the grandparents did survive, that bond succumbed to more pragmatic factors, for example, the fact that the grandparents were rarely fluent in the language of the countries where families settled, and the grandchildren rarely understood Yiddish. "Amnesia was a reality for those who stumbled on the edge of the void created by genocide. It was for this reason that Yizkor books remained unvisited cemeteries" (Wieviorka 1999, 130). This attempt at transmission, in both its form and content, did not succeed.[1]

> With street songs, theater, and rock songs, the young appeal to joy to think about the last military dictatorship. Without melancholia, they are looking for alternatives to speak about the tragic legacies of the past.

This is the headline of an article titled "Dancing on the Ashes" written by Patricia Rojas in the magazine *Puentes* (December 2000) about youth and memory in Argentina. Another headline celebrates the creativity of young people in their commemorative activities on dates associated with the military regime: "Graffiti, murals, and street singing are only some of the elements convened for the construction of memories." What the article affirms and reaffirms is that the young have "a different gaze at the past." It focuses on the activities organized by a specific group of young people, the children of the disappeared during the military dictatorship. These young people are highly visible in contemporary Argentina through the activism of the organization H.I.J.O.S. and through public demonstrations such as the one described above.[2] Several questions arise. What do "other" young people do? What meaning do they ascribe to the dictatorial past? And finally, when they search for "alternative ways," who is the other from whom they seek to differentiate themselves?

Social Temporality: Generations and Cohorts

> *[Generational replacement] serves the necessary social purpose of enabling us to forget. If society is to continue, social remembering is just as important as forgetting.*
>   Karl Mannheim, *Essays on the Sociology of Knowledge*

There is an evident fact: even as a member of the same social group—be it a small group, such as the family, up to humanity as a whole—the experience of living through a particular historical event is different depending on the age of the person. Living through a war at age five, at twenty-five, or at sixty produces very different subjective phenomena, as does whether one is close to where events take place or far away, and whether one is a man or a woman. Age, the moment in life when events take place, leaves specific marks because it affects life conditions, experiences, and future prospects. In collective or social terms, age—or in demographic terms, the birth cohort—also has another feature. It defines a collectivity, which also includes an imagined community, of people who share a set of historical opportunities and limitations that provide them, in a certain sense, with a "shared destiny."

What is at issue here is not only chronological age. Sharing a particular time (and space) in history predisposes the group "to a certain characteristic mode of thought and experience and a characteristic type of historically relevant action" (Mannheim 1952, 291). This is Mannheim's concept of *generation,* and he stresses that shared life experiences also imply a "shared destiny."

Besides its technical use in specialized books, the notion of generation is also present in common-sense thinking. We regularly speak of a Post-War Generation, the '68 Generation, or the generation that came of age under democratic rule.[3] Their boundaries are always diffuse because they are social categories of experience shaped by temporality, but also by a shared arena of experience and some specific sense of belonging (literary generations or political ones are cases in point). National identities may at times be the boundaries of the generational imagined community, although often national boundaries are crossed by transnational generational groups—the '68 Generation and the Beatles Generation (which in part overlap each other) were truly transnational, not to mention the generations coming of age in the context of contemporary globalization and its impact on networks of communications and belonging.

The succession of generations—in the demographic sense of the replacement of one generation by another—is closely related to processes of social memory. What traces of the past are irrevocably erased? Which remain active or dormant in oblivion, only to be recuperated in the future? How does the work of "memory entrepreneurs" intervene in the actualization and renewal of recollections and in the meanings of the past themselves?

In fact, the operation of multiple temporalities implies diverse processes of transformation. First there is personal growth, maturation, and aging. The life course is an inexorable process. In each person, moreover, both new experiences and the horizon of future expectations change over time. Memories of lived events, lapses and amnesias, and the feelings involved in them also change. The sense of urgency that motivates work around legacies and memory projects, and around the conservation of its traces, is also transformed in time. When reaching old age, many want to "transmit," to convey and leave something of their experiences for future generations.

Second is the temporality of historical time itself. Public events and historical processes take place in and over time, transecting institutional, demographic, political, and other dynamics. The flow of historical time is the result of the goals and expectations of human groups, carried into action under circumstances and conditions that they generally do not control and with consequences that are not always intended. Yet these are also men and women who grow, mature, age, and die. This leads us to a third temporality, that of the generational succession and replacement of historical agents. Institutions may operate within a time frame of *la longue durée,* but their social location, their significance, and their personnel are under constant renovation (although in certain instances some figures may become "eternalized," demonstrating that aging is not necessarily an obstacle to decades of permanence within a particular institution. I think here of Franco, Stroessner, or John Paul II).

The Lessons and Apprehensions of the Past

As I have already pointed out, memory provides a link between past experiences and future expectations. It is past experiences that remain, that are forgotten, and that are transformed in the interplay between present circumstances and expectations for the future. A question that immediately arises here is whether we can actually learn from the past. What would be the dynamics of that learning process? What are the "lessons of history"? What is at issue here? A re-presentation of the past or other means by which past experience is captured?

The issue of the uses of memory for the present and future, of the lessons and legacies that may be gleaned from the past, can be approached from a number of different perspectives. From a cognitive approach, knowing something, having previously learned it, has implications for the strategies in which rational alternatives for action are worked out. From a psychoanalytic perspective, the past is in the present, in multiple forms, and is subject to the dynamics of the unconscious. A cultural perspective would emphasize the meanings ascribed to the past, considering the interpretive framework and cultural codes that enable its interpretation—in rational and systematic terms or within the symbolic and performative practices of actors who more than re-presenting or remembering, appropriate the past and enact it in the present.[4]

The notion that the past can be learned from is implicit in the logic that guides the political activity of those who propose slogans such as "Never Again," or "Remember so as not to repeat." This notion is also present in studies dealing with changing political systems and particularly with processes of democratization.

What can be learned from the past? Paloma Aguilar Fernández applies the notion of political learning to the Spanish democratization process. Her argument starts by establishing that people tend to learn more from their own experiences than from those of others.[5] The conclusion she draws from this "weight of the past" in connection with the Spanish Civil War is that "generational replacement was necessary, perhaps indispensable, particularly if we take into account that we had to deal with a dramatic and difficult past, plagued by poorly healed wounds" (Aguilar Fernández 1996, 52). Furthermore, in terms of the life course of social actors, the events that leave the most profound marks are those that take place early in life and those that happen when subjects begin to gain awareness of the political arenas of which they are part, which implies posing a "delayed effect" of political learning and the lessons learned. The implementation of the lessons of history takes at least twenty years—approximately the time it takes for a new generation to come to power (Aguilar Fernández 1996, 53).[6] In the case of the Spanish transition, the central lesson that the new generation brought to the political arena was the notion of "never again" to violent and traumatic confrontations, which required the production and "use" of political amnesia and silences. However, these open political silences, which showed up in the willingness of diverse political actors to negotiate and to reach agreements, were accompanied by a wide range of symbolic expressions of the memories of the past—of the Republic, of the Civil War, of the Franco regime and its diverse modes of repression—particularly in the cultural field (literature, film, and so on).

In the countries of the Southern Cone, the dictatorships were generally shorter than the Franco regime in Spain, explaining why there was no generational change among political actors. The transitions in the 1980s and 1990s took place in a different international context, one where the issue of human rights had gained greater primacy and new meanings. Under these new circumstances (and without ignoring the specific conditions of the political struggles in each country), efforts to negotiate and achieve consensus between authoritarian actors and the proponents of transition—based on covering the past with "a mantle of oblivion," abrogating responsibilities through amnesty laws, or emphasizing the construction of a "promising future"—were not very successful and ended up being unstable.

Demands for institutional solutions that include "truth and justice" remain strong after more than a decade since transition. These voices obstinately confront those who ask for "reconciliation" and oblivion. In such contexts, the question regarding the possible change that generational succession may bring about remains open. New generations may arrive to the political stage with alternative views, based in part on the lessons of past experiences (rejecting armed struggle, for example), while at the same time they may reawaken memories, questioning their elders about their commitments and their experiences in the conflictive and repressive past.

Memory as Tradition and as Transmission

Yosef Yerushalmi (1996) argues that, in a strict and purely individual sense, one can only forget the events that one has lived through. What was not lived through cannot be forgotten:

> When we say that a people "remembers" we are really saying that a past has been actively transmitted to the present generation and that this past has been accepted as meaningful. Conversely, a people "forgets" when the generation that now possesses the past does not convey it to the next, or when the latter rejects what it receives and does not pass it onward, which is to say the same thing. . . . A people can never "forget" what it has never received in the first place. (109)

Here the author poses a central issue, that of the transmission between those who lived through an event and those who did not, either because they had not yet been born, because they were not present where the event took place, or because even though they were nearby or in the scenario of action, they experienced it differently due to their age or their social place.

There are traditions and customs, "the complex of rites and beliefs that gives a people its sense of identity and purpose" (Yerushalmi 1996, 113), which are transmitted and incorporated by successive generations without much explicit effort or planning. Traditional institutions such as the church and the family, social classes and the nation served as "the social frameworks of memory" for a long time, as Maurice Halbwachs has suggested. This long-term social function is being sharply altered in contemporary times, in an era of accelerating temporal rhythms, of multiple and deterritorialized modes of communication and contact, and of plural spaces of belonging, all of which imply asking questions about established or even sacralized beliefs. As a consequence, many may mourn the passing of tradition, of the Law, of *halakhah*—an issue that concerns both Pierre Nora and Yerushalmi, among others.

We live in a time when traditions are subject to multiple forms of critical scrutiny, when hierarchical paradigms based on canonical knowledge are undergoing profound transformations, and in which a plurality of new subjects are demanding their place within the public sphere. In this context, the transmission of the knowledge and meanings of the past becomes an open and public issue, subject to strategic struggles and controversies about the "politics of memory." Thus, besides taking the multiplicity of actors and the diversity of their experiences and interpretations of the past into account, the issue of memory transmission unfolds in several layers simultaneously, which can reinforce each other, remain disarticulated, or even contradict each other. There is, first, the social inertia of processes of transmission of traditions and accumulated social knowledge; second, the strategic actions of "memory entrepreneurs" who develop active policies of meanings of the past; and third, the processes of intergenerational transmission.

Psychoanalysis has closely examined the dynamics of intergenerational transmission, showing that the impulse or the urgency to convey to others originates in a need brought about by unconscious energies that respond to narcissistic demands, a necessity of transmitting "what cannot be maintained or sheltered within the subject himself" (Kaës 1996). Transmission is not only organized through visible or manifest means but also through silences and particularly through voids and lapses. The mechanisms of identification with the parental figures are fundamental in this process; so is the ability of the subject to achieve autonomy (Faimberg 1996).[7] As Jacques Hassoun (1996) points out,

> Successful transmission offers he or she who receives it a space of freedom and a foundation that allows that person to *abandon (the past) in order to (better) reencounter it.* (17)

"Active" Memories

Let us return to memories and subjects. In everyday language, there is a widespread common-sense understanding of the notion of "intergenerational transmission" of behavioral patterns, of values, of information and knowledge. At one level, this transmission can be seen as part of the basic mechanisms of social and cultural reproduction. First the family and then other institutions play a direct and active role in the *socialization* of the new generations. Cultural transmission between one generation and the next, however, cannot be reduced to the reproduction of patterns of action and the creation of varied forms of belonging. With modernity and the demands for cultural democratization, the expectation and presupposition of the socialization process are that what is to be developed are reflexive subjects, who have gained the ability to choose and organize their own lives. This means that there will always be discontinuities and endogenous innovations, along with those generated by historical dynamics itself, since the transmission of reflexivity undermines the automatic transmission of the social models for explicit behavior.

What are we talking about then? Who does the transmitting, and what is being transmitted? To whom? What do those who are supposed to receive the transmission incorporate? To convey the meanings of the past, there are at least two prerequisites. First, there needs to be a basis for the process of identification, for an intergenerational expansion of the "we." Second, the possibility that those who are on the receiving end will reinterpret and resignify whatever is being conveyed has to be left open. It will never be a process of simple repetition or memorizing. In fact, this second prerequisite points to the need for new generations to learn how to approach the subjects and experiences of the past as "others," as different from their own, and to be willing to engage in a dialogue rather than simply re-present that past through a direct identification with it. As soon as the subjective level is taken into consideration, there is no way to prevent or block reinterpretations, resignifications, and new readings of the past, because the "same" history and the "same" truth inevitably acquire alternative meanings when the context has changed. And the succession of cohorts or generations necessarily implies the emergence of new contexts.

There is yet another mechanism that common sense takes for granted: to link or associate given patterns of behavior with the availability or absence of information. If people only "knew," the story goes, they would change their attitudes and their practices. The people who believe in this notion then elaborate strategies to "transmit" information and knowledge. Perhaps the insistence on the necessity to "remember so as not to forget" can also be interpreted in these terms. The complaints are heard everywhere: that the young do not know what happened on March 24, 1976, in Argentina, that they do not know who Pinochet was, that they do not know the history of the Shoah.

Yet the issue here is not simply the accumulation of knowledge. First of all, knowledge is not made up of loose objects that can be piled up or simply accumulated. Knowledge only has meaning within shared interpretive frameworks. Following this path, the social demands to bring particular versions or narratives of the past into the public sphere, or the demands to include specific facts about the past in curricular textbooks or in the "official history" have a dual motivation. One is explicit and is linked to the transmission of a specific meaning of the past to new generations. The other is implicit, although no less important, and responds to the urgency of legitimating and institutionalizing the public recognition of a particular narrative memory in contrast to others. These processes never involve "neutral" facts or histories but are rather imbued with particular social mandates. Such memories attain a formative or educational significance when they can be interpreted in "exemplary" terms (Todorov 1998).

Controversies of this sort are present all over the world. The political controversy in Japan over sexual slavery of women during World War II reached its peak with the decision of the Ministry of Education in June 1996 to include a reference to these abuses in school textbooks. That decision immediately incited responses from the Right, which, shrouded in a kind of scientific historicism, retorted that there was no documentation that established that the Japanese state had given the order to create this system of sexual slavery, and that it was inappropriate to transmit anything that did not meet the strictest standards of (positivist) historiography. The testimonial evidence and other "data" about the phenomenon's existence were not sufficient (Sand 1999; see also Yoneyama 1999).[8]

The debate about how to include recent history in education curricula has also taken place in the Southern Cone. Attempts to introduce dates of commemoration in curricular calendars, during which teachers are to impart special classes on the events in question, or even attempts to eliminate commemorative dates established by military regimes (such as September 11 in Chile, which was abolished as a national holiday only in 1999) generally come from social sectors linked to human rights movements. These are resisted by conservative forces and at times even by teachers themselves. They may believe that such initiatives touch upon issues that remain socially conflictive, and about which there is no social consensus. In some cases, there is not even agreement on what to call the events in question.[9] (There are also instrumental considerations, since teachers are rarely provided the necessary materials to prepare these classes). In-depth studies focusing specifically on the incorporation of such issues into the educational system will probably show that these processes have a very strong institutional component, since they require reaching a minimum degree of consensus and an institutionally legitimized version of what took place. If the political conflict is not yet resolved, it is impossible to elaborate such a version of past events. In such contexts, the educational system becomes yet another arena in which different actors and narratives struggle over memory and the meanings of the past.

Very often, the strategies of transmission of right-wing ideologues have enjoyed more success. Simplified Manichaean schemes without "gray areas" or fissures are more easily transmitted than interpretations that are polysemous and that allow for multiple meanings and interpretations. As Alessandro Portelli (1997, 1999) demonstrates in the case of the memory of the resistance in Italy, the discourse of the right-wing has succeeded in transforming into common sense the interpretation that the massacres of the Nazis were usually in response to attacks by Italian partisans, a framework that shifts responsibility for many "innocent deaths" from the Nazis onto partisan forces.

The issue of the transmission of information about the past also has its opposite side—specifically, the risk of oversaturation:

> As someone born in the Netherlands in 1958 into a non-Jewish family, who passed through primary and high school in the 1960's and early 1970's in the same country, I had the memory of the Second World War and the Holocaust drummed into my mind. Or rather, the Dutch school system and representations in the media tried to do so. But they failed to have the required effect. I was bored to death by all the stories and images of that war, which were held out to me "of-

ficially" as moral warnings. . . . My resistance to teachings about the war and the Holocaust requires explanation. To which aspects did I overreact so vehemently? Why was I bored instead of feeling morally addressed? (van Alphen 1997, 1)

In this autobiographical reflection, the author raises several points of interest. First, the stories of the war bored him because they did not leave room to elaborate any kind of response. The "appropriate" responses were already culturally scripted and programmed. There were no ambiguities; moral stances were crystallized and fixed. Second, there was an element of hypocrisy in the narratives. The heroic history being transmitted was not part of a ritual of mourning or of a lesson on moral sensitivity but rather a ritual confirmation of a triumphant nationalism. "As a person who was being told these stories I was not interpellated, to use Althusser's term, as a human being with moral responsibility, but as a young boy who had to construct his masculinity in the image of heroic fathers. That is why I felt bored: intuitively, I did not want to get involved with this cultural construction of a national, masculine identity" (van Alphen 1997, 2). Third, he could not integrate the Holocaust into the history of the war. There was no continuity between the episodes of war and the episodes of Jewish extermination. "Whereas the Holocaust was explained as being part of a more or less consistent, reconstructible history, to me it seemed like an intrusion of another world, one that did not relate to the war story of heroic masculinity. Unable to express my discomfort with the way that the Holocaust was embedded in the war narrative, I could only store the Holocaust images away" (3).[10]

This long citation allows us to raise a crucial issue regarding mechanisms of transmission: the limited role of historical and documentary discourses in educational attempts at transmission, and the place of the imaginative discourse of art and literature. In other words, the question is how to combine the transmission of information and knowledge, of ethical and moral principles, with the necessary stimulus for the development of distinct moods and sensibilities.[11]

Modern pedagogy bases its practices on the distinction between informational contents and "formative" practices. What matters in the latter are the more complex processes of identification with and appropriation of the past, and not only the transmission of information. As a consequence, the very idea of transmission, whether in more active or more passive manners, begins to break down.

Legacies, Remains, and Aftereffects

Let us return to the analytical distinction we have been exploring. Social actors and institutions can express a will to act (to preserve or transmit) vis-à-vis memory. The intention to bring justice may also be present, as well as the social recognition of the victims and the intent to educate toward the future. In practice, these three tasks are almost impossible to separate, although a certain path may be more successful in one direction or another (trials for the first, memorials and monuments for the second, educational materials for the third). In all these cases, what turns out to be crucial are the intentions, the will, and the strategic actions taken toward this triple objective. The idea of transmission and of leaving legacies (like that which is bestowed to someone through a will or testament) presupposes the inscription of meaning in messages that have been prepared with an *intention* of perpetuating and preserving.

These three intentionalities have been present in the actions of the human rights movement in the Southern Cone over the past fifteen years. The demand for justice was present from the initial moments of the transition, in spite of amnesty laws, and it persists over time. Commemorations, acknowledgment, and remembrance through plaques and monuments have been taking place since the moments of transition (Jelin 2002a; Jelin and Langland 2003). Debates about museums, archives, and academic research policies figure as well, although they may gain more force during a second stage (da Silva Catela and Jelin 2002).

Yet there is another level on which the memories of the past need to be examined, one that does not necessarily focus on the intentions of social actors but rather on the lessons and learnings, the remains, the practices and orientations that "are just there," whose origins may be traced, although less precisely, to the periods of repression and transition. These are the implicit legacies—the ritualized repetitions, the nostalgias and idealizations, the ruptures and fissures, and the scattered remains.

In 1978 the country was still living under what was called the "residual" authoritarianism—the brunt of the unhealthy legacy of the dictatorship—and this involved a heavy burden of fear and impulses of self-censorship. Censorship had already been officially eliminated from pressrooms, theaters, films, etc. But it had left something behind that, from my point of view as a journalist, was perhaps more pernicious than censorship itself. We had internalized all the paranoia and all the censorship. You did not need to have anyone beside you to inhibit or repress you . . . and this lasted a long time. For a long time we lived with this ghost, this shadow, this thing that hovered above us when it was time to write or to speak. (Ventura 1999, 130)

These are the thoughts of a Brazilian journalist reflecting upon an experience twenty years after the fact. Those ghosts and shadows continued to hover for a long time. For many, the aftereffects and remnants of an authoritarian period are not easily overcome, and they are present in everyday practices as automatic reactions—not leaving the house without carrying an identity card, feeling threatened, overreacting to the sound of sirens and uniforms. Along with voluntary silences, moreover, these are remnants of an earlier period, the traces of a past "that does not pass." Here what we encounter is not the insistence on public memory and recognition promoted by memory entrepreneurs but their opposite: traces and fragments, even in body language, that remain even when their origins and meanings have been forgotten. It is often new generations, those who did not live through the period that left these marks, who render them visible and ask questions about them.[12]

Norbert Lechner and Pedro Güell (1999) analyze the social construction of silence in the Chilean case. Framed by a politically negotiated and agreed upon transition, with institutional limits on the scope of the changes that could be made by the new regime, the issue of governance was at the center of the political stage. "Understanding governance more as an absence of conflicts than as a collective way to process them, the politics of memory does not help in chasing the ghosts of memory away: remembrance brings with it unmanageable conflicts. People do not find in the political realm the symbolic representations that could serve them as a mirror through which to name the past and thus apprehend it. Given this lack of words and symbols, they opt for silence. And memory opts to take hold of people through fear" (Lechner and Güell 1999, 194–95). The fears that Lechner (1999) identifies in contemporary Chilean society—fear of exclusion, of lack of meaning, of the other who is perceived as a potential aggressor—are linked to the "bad memory" or the "fear of memory." In this context, "the silenced conflicts [of the past] remain active in the present" (13).

We are faced here with the contrast between the intentionalities of memory entrepreneurs in the transmission of memories, and the traces and fragments left by the past. Legacies and inheritances assume that there is an active inscription of meaning with the *intent to preserve*. Testaments and wills are the medium through which actors attempt to convey to the next generation a significant link to a tradition and a lineage (Cardoso 1999, 135). In symbolic terms, a historical narrative is constructed and materialized and is then transmitted to others as the means to signal the continuity and permanence of a group or a community. When we speak of remnants, traces, or aftereffects, on the other hand, the reference is to the other face of memory, to the past returning, to oblivion and silences.[13]

Conclusion

Many open questions remain. In these concluding remarks, I want to take up an issue that, although frequently mentioned throughout the text, merits further discussion. The issue is that in addition to cultural and symbolic considerations, it is important to incorporate the analysis of institutions and the issues related to the democratic construction of citizenship. These issues are significant for an academic perspective; they are crucial and central for a book that wants to contribute to civic responsibility and action orientations.

A central institutional problem is the assignment of responsibilities for the repressive events of the past. Who should assume responsibility for the past? What does the recognition that there was state terrorism and state violations of human rights entail? Is it symbolic politics or actual policies of prosecution and reparation? Can the state and institutional actors foster a divide between the present—the democratic regime—and the past, which they do not recognize as their own? The political action of the state is always based on a principle of identity and historical continuity. Yet how does the state interpret dictatorial periods? As "disruptions" or as part of the continuity of state action (Booth 1999)?

The issue of the political identity of the state can, in the first place, be anchored in the political regime. Often, political regime changes are interpreted as radical changes, without recognizing the continuity with—and therefore state responsibility for—state actions in previous periods. In this perspective, official narratives highlight "foundational moments," even marking the ruptures in their own official nomenclature. The successive and numerous French and Spanish "Republics," the Brazilian "old" republic and the "New State," (Velha Republica and Estado Novo) are clear political examples of this kind. The German postwar regime and the debates about German responsibility for the Nazi period are also inscribed in this realm of tensions and conflicts. This solution of refoundations of the nation may be easy, but it is profoundly unsatisfying.[1]

At the state and collective level, the issue involved is again the relationship between memory and (national) identity. The dilemmas and tensions between universal and egalitarian citizenship, on the one hand, and community identity with the baggage of past memory, on the other, are present throughout this debate. Tensions between literal and exemplary memory, between individual and collective responsibility, between remembrance and oblivion are ever present. In institutional and citizenship terms, the tension can be expressed as one between a broad notion of open universal citizenship and the persistence of a community of remembrance, one that is exclusive and closed onto itself. The imperative of remembering and acting accordingly is the product of a community in which the past has moral presence in the present, based on the existence of a collective identity, an "us." In this context, forgetting, "especially if it is forgetting of our past injustices and our responsibilities for them (or of our past benefactors and our debt of grateful remembrance to them) savors of a wrong, of the violation of a duty, or, as Habermas writes, of the debt of atoning remembrance" (Booth 1999, 259). The ambiguity and tension between communities of memory, retrospective responsibilities, and a universalist vision of citizenship are quite evident. Rather than trying to give a simple formula for action, which would imply an authoritarian or authoritative approach to the matter, societies and social groups will find ways to handle the tension if they are placed in democratic public spaces and institutional settings that recognize the plurality of voices and the unavoidable presence of the past.

If we accept the premise of historical continuity, the question moves to another plane. How can the various conflicting memories of dictatorship and repression be articulated in democratic institutions and in open public spheres? The desired path seems not to entail attempting to impose one interpretation of the past or trying to build a (minimum) consensus among social and political actors. Rather, what seems clear is the necessity of legitimate spaces for the expression and controversy about different memories. A democratic order would imply, therefore, the recognition of plurality and conflict more than the hope for reconciliations, silences, or erasures by fiat. This recognition of conflict, however, has to be anchored strongly in the rule of law (Osiel 1997).

In sum, the strategy for incorporating the past calls for the creation of multiple spaces for debate. The educational system and the cultural domain are some of the spheres where a strategy for the critical incorporation of the past can be carried out. However, ultimately its meaning will be defined by the centrality of law and justice (Méndez, 1997). As Yosef Yerushalmi (1996) asks, "Is it possible that the antonym of 'forgetting' is not 'remembering,' but justice?" (117).

Appendix

A Chronology of Political Violence and Human Rights Movements

This section chronicles forty-eight years of political violence, state terrorism, institutional processes, and human rights movements in the Southern Cone (Argentina, Brazil, Chile, Paraguay, and Uruguay). The selection of events is not arbitrary, but like all chronologies this is just one of any number of different possible orderings of events. Nonetheless, it may help readers unfamiliar with the Southern Cone to set the historical context for processes of memory that are examined in the text.

The information is presented chronologically, then by country. It should be remembered that repressive regimes throughout the region coordinated their actions, as did the human rights movements that opposed them. The various groups engaged in peaceful and armed struggles to bring about revolutionary change and the democratically oriented political actors engaged in transitions to constitutional rule were also interconnected.

1954
Paraguay

May   General Alfredo Stroessner, Commander of the Army, leads a military coup.

August   Elections are held, and General Alfredo Stroessner becomes president, initiating thirty-five years of rule through repeated reelections (in 1958, 1963, 1968, 1973, 1978, 1983, and 1988), never fully free.

1958
Paraguay

August   Reelection of Stroessner as president, in elections with a single candidate.

1959
Paraguay

June   Stroessner dissolves parliament after students' protests are repressed.

1961
Brazil

August   President Janio Quadros resigns. Vice President Joao Goulart is sworn in as president amid considerable opposition.

1963
Paraguay

August   Stroessner begins his third presidential term, after elections in which an opposition candidate was allowed to run.

1964
Brazil

April 1   Military coup ousts President Joao Goulart, who seeks refuge in Uruguay. General Humberto Castelo Branco becomes president of the country on April 15.

June Creation of the SNI (Serviço Nacional de Inteligencia), aimed at advising and coordinating information and intelligence activities.

1967
Brazil

March Marechal Arturo da Costa e Silva becomes the second military president.

1968
Brazil

March Edson Luis, a university student, is shot by a policeman in Rio de Janeiro. Massive protests and workers' strikes follow in cities all over the country.

June The "rally of the 100,000" *(passeata dos 100 mil)* takes place in Rio de Janeiro, the largest gathering against the military government since the 1964 coup.

December The government dissolves congress and issues the *Ato Institucional N° 5,* giving total control of the country to the president. Public gatherings are prohibited, censorship is imposed, and civil liberties are suspended.

Paraguay

February–August Constitutional Convention accepts new reelections of the president.

August Reelection of Alfredo Stroessner as president.

Uruguay

August Police kill student Liber Arce in a street rally. This is one of the first acts of open political violence with a fatal casualty. Liber Arce will later become an emblem of victims of state repression.

1969
Brazil

August   President Costa e Silva suffers a stroke and is replaced by a military junta.

September   U.S. Ambassador to Brazil Charles Burke Elbrick
is kidnapped by the revolutionary group MR-8.

October   General Emilio Garrastazú Medici becomes
president.

Uruguay

October   A MLNT (Movimiento de Liberación Nacional
Tupamaros [The Tupamaro Movement for National Liberation]) commando takes control of
the city of Pando for one hour, as a show of their
organizational abilities and their power.

1970
Chile

September   Socialist Salvador Allende Gossens is elected president by a slim margin of votes. Congress confirms
his election in October.

December   Allende nationalizes the Chilean copper industry.

Uruguay

July   The MLNT kidnaps Dan Mitrione, a U.S. advi-
sor (implicated in training the Uruguayan military
in repressive techniques), and kills him after the
government refuses to negotiate the terms of his
release.

1971
Uruguay

September   After the escape of Tupamaro prisoners from a
Montevideo prison, the president calls on the
armed forces to take responsibility for the "anti-
subversive" struggle.

October   The MLNT declares a six-month electoral truce.

1972
Chile

October A massive strike by truck drivers and owners para-
lyzes the country and intensifies conflicts between
Allende supporters and the opposition.

Uruguay

March Juan M. Bordaberry is sworn in as president.
Elections were held in November 1971.

April 14 The MLNT executes four state officials accused
of belonging to the Escuadrón de la muerte (Death
Squadron). Eight members of the MLNT are killed
in retaliation.

April A "State of Internal War" is declared. Individual
rights and guarantees are suspended.

July A law of state security is passed by congress, by
which all citizens are subject to military justice.

1973
Argentina

May Héctor Cámpora is sworn in as president.
Elections were held in March.

June Juan D. Perón returns from exile in Spain. There
are violent confrontations between factions of the
Peronist movement in Ezeiza, while waiting for his
arrival.

July President Cámpora resigns.

September Juan D. Perón is elected president and sworn into
office.

Chile

March Allende's Popular Unity coalition increases its
electoral support in legislative and municipal
elections.

June Several army regiments participate in a failed coup
attempt.

September 11 Army Commander-in-Chief General Augusto
Pinochet leads a coup, with air raids on the

presidential palace. President Salvador Allende dies in the presidential palace during the attack.

October   The ecumenical Comité de Cooperación Para la Paz (Committee for Peace) is created to defend human rights.

Paraguay

February   Reelection of Alfredo Stroessner as president.

Uruguay

June   In a military-civilian coup, Parliament is dissolved and replaced by a State Council, empowering the armed forces and police to take whatever measures are necessary to ensure normal public services. President Bordaberry is kept in office.

July   A general strike and massive rally against the coup are fiercely repressed. Liber Seregni, leader of the opposition Frente Amplio, is imprisoned. Wilson Ferreira Aldunate (leader of the Partido Nacional) takes the road of exile.

1974
Argentina

July   President Perón dies. His wife and vice president María E. Martínez de Perón takes office. Afterwards, armed guerrilla operations take place in various parts of the country. Paramilitary forces, among them the Triple A (Argentine Anticommunist Alliance), terrorize the country.

Brazil

March   General Ernesto Geisel becomes president. He introduces reforms that allow limited political activity and elections—the beginnings of the so-called *abertura*.

November   Congressional elections. The opposition party MDB gains control of the senate.
During 1974, the Movimento Feminino pela Anistía is created.

Chile

June   The DINA (Dirección de Inteligencia Nacional, in charge of intelligence and repression) is established. Pinochet is designated as Supreme Head of the Nation.

Argentina-Chile

September 30   Chile's former Army Commander-in-Chief Carlos Prats, a strong opponent of Pinochet, is assassinated in Buenos Aires alongside his wife.

1975
Argentina

February   The government initiates the Operativo Independencia, ordering army troops to combat armed guerrillas in the province of Tucumán.

November   The army is assigned the task of "annihilating" armed guerrilla movements.

December   The *Asamblea Permanente de los Derechos Humanos* (Permanent Human Rights Assembly) is created.
Political violence is rampant throughout the year.

Brazil

October   Journalist Vladimir Herzog is murdered when under detention. Massive memorial service is held.

Chile

November   Under pressure from the regime, the Comité de Cooperación Para la Paz is dissolved.

Uruguay

August   April 14 is designated as the "Día de los caídos en la lucha contra la sedición" (Day of the fallen in the struggle against sedition).

December   President Bordaberry cancels scheduled elections and abolishes political parties.

1976
Argentina

March 24 Military coup. A military junta is formed to direct the Proceso de Reorganización Nacional (Process of National Reorganization, as the military government designated itself). General Jorge Videla is named president.

Throughout the year, various groups and human rights-related organizations become active, among them Movimiento Ecuménico de Derechos Humanos (Ecumenical Human Rights Movement) and Familiares de desaparecidos y detenidos por razones políticas (Relatives of the Disappeared and Prisoners for Political Reasons).

Argentina-Uruguay

May 20 Uruguayan ex-senator Zelmar Michelini and ex-speaker of the house Hector Gutiérrez Ruiz are assassinated in Buenos Aires.

Argentina-Brazil

May Brazilian ex-president Joao Goulart dies in Argentina, presumably of a heart attack. In 2000, after denunciations that he was murdered as part of the Operativo Cóndor, an investigative commission was formed in Brazil to collect evidence about the circumstances of his death.

Uruguay

June Civilian president J. M. Bordaberry is overthrown. After an interim period, in September General Aparicio Méndez is chosen by a military-civilian national council as president. *Acto Institucional Nº4* bans some fifteen thousand citizens from engaging in political activity for fifteen years.

Chile

January The Vicaría de la Solidaridad is created, replacing the Comité de Cooperación para la Paz.

January The Inter-American Human Rights Committee of the Organization of American States condemns human rights violations in Chile.

September Orlando Letelier, exiled former foreign minister and ambassador to the United States, is murdered by a car bomb in Washington, D.C.

1977
Argentina

April The Asamblea Permanente de Derechos Humanos makes the first massive presentation of Habeas Corpus.

April First meeting of the Madres de Plaza de Mayo (mothers of the disappeared).

August Patricia Derian, Human Rights Secretary in the Carter administration, meets with General Videla.

October The Abuelas de Plaza de Mayo begin their collective search for their kidnapped grandchildren.

December Eleven relatives of disappeared people (including the leader of the Madres de Plaza de Mayo) and two French nuns disappear.

Brazil

January Manifesto is signed by more than one thousand intellectuals protesting against censorship.

April The federal government closes congress. During the two-week recess, decrees are implemented (the *Pacote de Abril*) aimed at strengthening the institutional control of the ruling group.

July–September Students' protests are answered with repression.

Chile

August In response to international pressures, DINA is dissolved and substituted with the CNI (Central Nacional de Informaciones). The government engages in plans for constitutional reform.

Uruguay

June–July Institutional repression intensifies as the government takes direct control of the judiciary.

1978

Argentina

June   Soccer World Cup in Argentina. The human rights organizations ask for solidarity of international journalists.

Brazil

March–   First strikes in the industrial areas of Sao Paulo.
November   The strike movement will grow until September, when a ban on union meetings is decreed by the government. Luis Ignacio da Silva (Lula), who will be the founder of the Partido Trabalhista and be elected president in 2002, is the president of the metallurgical union of Sao Bernardo do Campo.

December   Formal end of *Ato Institutional N° 5*, established in 1968. However, many of its provisions will continue in the future.
Throughout the year, growing societal demands of a political amnesty coalesce in the Comité Brasileiro pela Anistía.

Chile

April   Amnesty law pardons violations committed between September 1973 and March 1978 (by state agents and by dissidents).

November   Remains of fifteen disappeared persons are discovered in Lonquén.

Paraguay

February   Reelection of Alfredo Stroessner as president.

1979

Argentina

August   The Madres de Plaza de Mayo become a formal organization.

September   The Inter-American Commission of Human Rights of the Organization of American States (OAS) visits Argentina to investigate human rights violations.

Brazil

March Lula leads a major strike of industrial workers in the area of Sao Paulo. The government intervenes in the unions and dismisses union leadership.

March President Joao Baptista Figueiredo takes office. He promises to continue along the path toward political liberalization.

May First Students' Union (UNE) Congress after the end of *Ato Institucional 5*.

August An amnesty law is approved. Political detainees are freed, and exiles begin to return.

November Congress approves a law-reforming party structure, allowing for a limited multiparty system.

Paraguay

The opposition front Acuerdo Nacional (the National Accord) is formed.

1980

Argentina

March Creation of CELS (Centro de Estudios Legales y Sociales [Center for Legal and Social Studies]), an organization offering legal assistance to relatives of the disappeared.

August A large public rally of relatives of the disappeared takes place in Buenos Aires.

October Adolfo Pérez Esquivel, leader of SERPAJ *(Servicio Paz y Justicia)*, receives the Nobel Peace Prize.

December The first *Marcha de la resistencia* (March of Resistance), a twenty-four-hour rally, takes place in Buenos Aires. The march will become an annual event.

Brazil

March–September Bomb attacks in many public places (including newsstands and lawyers' offices) linked to the opposition to the military government.

April Strike in the industrial area of Sao Paulo. Lula and other union leaders are jailed.

Chile

September 11   New constitution is approved in a plebiscite.

Uruguay

November   A proposed constitutional reform that gives the military a virtual veto power over all governmental policies is rejected in a plebiscite. A complex process of transition to constitutional rule is opened up by this rejection.

1981

Argentina

March   General Roberto Eduardo Viola becomes president, replacing Jorge R. Videla.

December   An internal reshuffling of the military junta results in General Leopoldo Fortunato Galtieri becoming president.

Brazil

April 30   A bomb explodes in a car in the parking lot during a popular musical show in the Riocentro hall, with twenty thousand people in attendance. A military sergeant dies inside the car, and an army officer is seriously injured.

July   Military justice officials ask to dismiss the investigation of the bomb, claiming that there is not sufficient evidence. There will be attempts to reopen the investigation of the *"episodio Riocentro"* beginning in 1985.

August   A cabinet crisis linked to the Riocentro case leads to the resignation of General Golberi de Couto e Silva as head of the civilian cabinet.

September   President Figueiredo is hospitalized with a stroke. Vice President Aureliano Chaves replaces him. Figueiredo will resume office in November.

Chile

March   General Augusto Pinochet is sworn in as president for another eight years. He takes possession of

La Moneda Presidential Palace after completing repairs and renovation (due to the damage of the September 11, 1973, bombing).

September 11   The new constitution is enacted.

Uruguay

September   General Gregorio Alvarez Armellino is named president.

1982

Argentina

March   Labor unions and political parties protest in the first national strike since the beginning of the dictatorship. The answer is violent street repression.

April   The armed forces invade the Malvinas (Falkland Islands), leading to war with the United Kingdom. The Argentine armed forces surrender in June.

July   General Reynaldo Bignone assumes the presidency. The longstanding ban on political activities is lifted.

December   Massive demonstration takes place against dictatorship.

Street rallies and protests are repressed throughout the year.

Brazil

November   National elections for congress and state governors. The opposition gains the majority of the Chamber of Deputies, but the official party maintains the majority in the Electoral College that will elect the next president.

Uruguay

Internal elections are held in political parties. In all of them, the winners are the groups opposing military rule.

1983

Argentina

April   The military issue their "final document," an institutional act declaring that all those who fought against terrorism are exempt from punishment on the grounds that such operations are to be considered "acts of service" to the nation.

September   The military government passes a "self-amnesty" law.

September–
December   Multiple rallies and marches protest the "self-amnesty" law and call for the reappearance of the disappeared and for punishment for the perpetrators *(Aparición con vida y castigo a los culpables)*.

October   Free national elections are held. Raúl Alfonsín is elected president.

December   Raúl Alfonsín takes office as president and announces several decrees and law proposals addressing human rights violations, including (a) repeal of the "self-amnesty" law, (b) arrest and prosecution of the members of the three military juntas and the most important leaders of the guerrilla movements, (c) the creation of the CONADEP (Comisión nacional sobre Desaparición de Personas [National Commission concerning the Disappeared Persons]), and (d) reforms to the military code.

Brazil

June   A national campaign for direct elections is launched by the opposition parties. The campaign gains supporters and organizes marches and rallies all over the country during the following months.

Chile

May   First national protest against the regime. Monthly protests (on the 11 of each month) last until 1985. They are violently repressed.

Paraguay

February   Reelection of Alfredo Stroessner as president.

Uruguay

May   After ten years of prohibition and repression, first street rally in commemoration of Workers' Day.

November   Massive political rally demanding elections with full restoration of democratic norms and without political proscriptions.

1984

Argentina

February   A law reforming the military code is approved by the legislature, with the proviso that sentences imposed by military courts are to be automatically appealed through federal courts.

September   The military courts refuse to prosecute ex-military commanders.

September   CONADEP presents its report (*Nunca Más* [Never Again]) to the president, registering 8,900 cases of forced disappearance and documenting the operation of more than three hundred clandestine detention centers.

Brazil

April   High point of the *"Diretas já"* campaign, which started in November 1983, demanding direct presidential elections. Street rallies all over the country involve millions of people (close to 1 million in Rio de Janeiro, 1.7 million in Sao Paulo).

April   The proposed constitutional amendment to allow for direct presidential elections is defeated in congress. Elections will be through an electoral college.

Uruguay

March   Liber Seregni is released from prison.

June   Wilson Ferreira Aldunate returns to the country from exile.

July–August   Military and civilian political leaders meet in a dialogue to negotiate the transition. The *Pacto del Club Naval* is agreed upon.

November   National elections. The Partido Colorado candidate Julio María Sanguinetti is elected.

1985

Argentina

April   The trial of the nine ex-military commanders begins in the federal court of Buenos Aires.

December   The federal court sentences five of the nine ex-commanders in chief of the Armed Forces to prison terms that range from four years to life. Four members of the juntas are acquitted.

Brazil

January   Tancredo Neves is elected first civilian president in twenty-one years under the electoral college system set up by the military.

March   Tancredo Neves falls ill before taking office, and his vice president José Sarney is sworn in as president.

April   Death of Tancredo Neves.

October   After attempts to reopen the judicial inquiry about the Riocentro case, the Supreme Military Tribunal (Superior Tribunal Militar) calls for closing the case.

Uruguay

March 1   President Julio María Sanguinetti takes office. An amnesty law for political prisoners is enacted.

April 14   Sanguinetti changes the name of the day to "Día de los caídos en defensa de las instituciones democráticas" (Day of the fallen in defense of democratic institutions).

May 20   Street rally commemorating the assassination of Michelini and Gutiérrez Ruiz.

1986
Argentina

January The Madres de Plaza de Mayo divide. The two groups are subsequently known as the Asociación Madres de Plaza de Mayo and Madres de Plaza de Mayo-Línea Fundadora.

Throughout the year, unrest builds within the armed forces in response to the continuing prosecutions for human rights violations.

December Congress passes the *Ley de Punto Final* (Full Stop Law), limiting prosecutions of members of the armed forces.

Brazil

November Elections are held for senators and deputies that will form the National Constitutional Assembly.

December An official commission is created to investigate the disappearance of 125 persons during the military regime.

Chile

September Augusto Pinochet narrowly escapes an assassination attempt.

Uruguay

December An amnesty law is approved in parliament *(Ley de caducidad de la pretensión punitiva del Estado)*.

1987
Argentina

April Military upheaval of Easter weekend.

May Congress passes the *Ley de Obediencia Debida* (Due Obedience Law), banning prosecution of members of the armed forces when they acted following orders.

Brazil

February   The National Constitutional Assembly begins its work toward a new federal constitution.

September   The Council for the Defense of Human Rights (Conselho de Defesa dos Direitos Humanos) approves the request to reopen the Riocentro case, based on new evidence given by testimony of one of the participants in the bombing.

Uruguay

January   Creation of the Comisión Nacional Pro-Referendum (National Commission Pro-referendum) to ask for a referendum repealing the amnesty law. In December, the more than five hundred thousand signatures needed to implement the referendum are presented.

1988
Argentina

January   Military rebellion in Monte Caseros.
December   Military rebellion in Villa Martelli.

Brazil

October   The new constitution is approved, allowing for direct presidential elections.

Chile

October   Pinochet loses the national plebiscite. Voters reject his plan to remain in power eight more years.

Paraguay

February   Reelection of Alfredo Stroessner as president.

1989
Argentina

The Movimiento Todos por la Patria, a group linked to past armed guerrilla groups, attempts to assault an army camp, the Regimiento 13 in La Tablada. A bloody repression follows.

May   Carlos Saúl Menem is elected president.

July   Menem is sworn in as president earlier than expected, following the resignation of President Alfonsín.

October   President Menem enacts the first presidential pardon benefiting, among others, military perpetrators of human rights violations and some leaders of the armed guerrilla movement. Massive rallies protest the presidential pardons.

December   Military rebellion is repressed and controlled.

December   Menem announces a second presidential pardon, including the convicted and imprisoned members of the military juntas.

Chile

December   Patricio Aylwin is elected president, after seventeen years of military rule.

Paraguay

February   A military coup ousts General Stroessner. He resigns and escapes to Brazil.

May   General Andrés Rodríguez is elected president in the first free elections in thirty-five years.

Paraguay-Brazil

February   Brazil grants political asylum to Stroessner.

Uruguay

March   Presentation of the report *Uruguay Nunca Más,* prepared by human rights organizations (SERPAJ). It reports the highest rate of political prisoners in the Southern Cone, and 166 cases of forced disappearances.

April   The human rights movement is defeated in a referendum called to approve or reject the amnesty law.

1990

Brazil

March   Fernando Collor de Mello is sworn in as president. His election is the first direct presidential election in more than a quarter century (elections took place in December 1989).

March   One of the first governmental measures is closing the SNI (Serviço Nacional de Inteligencia).

Chile

February   The CNI (Central Nacional de Informaciones [National Center of Information]) is abolished.

March   Patricio Aylwin is sworn in as president.

April   The Comisión Nacional por la Verdad y la Reconciliación (National Truth and Reconciliation Commission) is created.

September   State funeral for Salvador Allende.

September   The Memorial to the Disappeared and Executed is inaugurated in the Santiago General Cemetery.

Uruguay

March 1   Luis Alberto Lacalle is sworn in as president.

1991

Brazil

May   Commemorating the tenth anniversary of the bombs in Riocentro, the press deals extensively with the issue of the military responsibility. Based on this coverage, new requests to reopen the case are presented.

Chile

March   The National Truth and Reconciliation Commission (known as the Rettig Commission) presents its report. The report presents information on more than 2,200 deaths and disappearances due to state repression during the dictatorship. President Aylwin formally asks relatives of the victims for forgiveness and calls for gestures from the military acknowledging the pain and suffering inflicted.

1992
Argentina

March   A bomb destroys the Israeli Embassy in Buenos Aires.

Brazil

May   Congress establishes an investigating committee to deal with allegations of corruption of President Collor de Mello.

August   First street rallies asking for the impeachment of President Collor de Mello.

October   President Collor de Mello is temporarily removed from office by congress, pending impeachment procedures. Vice President Itamar Franco becomes interim president.

December   Impeachment procedures come to a close, with the condemnation of Collor de Mello.

Paraguay

June   New constitution is approved after the elected Constitutional Convention introduced participatory mechanisms in its deliberations. The new constitution includes *Habeas Data* provisions.

December   The archives of Stroessner's secret police are discovered in Asunción. Documents show the workings of Paraguayan repression and document the Operativo Cóndor.

1993
Chile

December   Eduardo Frei Ruiz-Tagle is elected president.

Paraguay

Juan Carlos Wasmosi is elected president.

1994
Argentina

July   A bomb destroys the Jewish community center (AMIA) in Buenos Aires.

August   The elected Constitutional Convention reforms the constitution, allowing for presidential reelection. The new constitution incorporates all international treaties on human rights as constitutional text.

The children of the disappeared, imprisoned, and exiled (now in their early twenties) start meeting and organizing themselves.

1995
Argentina

March   First public confessions of military perpetrators, with wide media coverage.

April   The commander-in-chief of the army, General Martín Balza, condemns the actions of the armed forces during the military regime.

May   Carlos Menem is reelected.

October   The organization H.I.J.O.S. (Hijos por la identidad, la justicia, contra el olvido y el silencio [Sons and Daughters for Identity, Justice, against Forgetting and Silence]) is created.

Brazil

January   Fernando Henrique Cardoso is sworn in as president (elections took place in October 1994).

March   The Chamber of Deputies creates a special committee for human rights (Comissão dos Direitos Humanos).

August   On the sixteenth anniversary of the amnesty law, the government sends to congress a law proposal establishing economic reparations for the relatives of the disappeared and the dead.

Chile

June   Manuel Contreras is sentenced, in absentia, to twenty years in prison by an Italian court for ordering the 1975 attempted assassination in Rome of Bernardo Leighton.

Uruguay

March 1 José M. Sanguinetti is sworn in as president for the
second time.

1996
Argentina

March Massive rallies commemorate the twentieth anniversary of the military coup.
H.I.J.O.S. becomes very active and visible through
their *escraches,* a form of public gathering designed to denounce and shame perpetrators.

December Abuelas de Plaza de Mayo present a case in the
criminal courts against child kidnapping and appropriation.
Spanish and Italian courts begin prosecutorial
inquiries related to human rights violations in
Argentina. These inquiries expand then to Chile
and Uruguay.

Brazil

On the basis of press reports and published tes-
timony, the Congressional Committee of Human
Rights asks the attorney general to reopen the
Riocentro case.

Paraguay

April Attempted coup by General Lino Oviedo, who
does not accept his retirement. The coup is averted.

Uruguay

May Navy Captain (ret.) Jorge Tróccoli admits to having participated in repressive activities, marking
the first public recognition of guilt on the part of a
perpetrator.

May 20 First "silence rally" organized by the Asociación
de Familiares de Desaparecidos (Association of
Relatives of the Disappeared) demanding information about the fate of the disappeared. Similar rallies have taken place annually ever since.

1997
Argentina

Several court cases linked to kidnapping and illegal appropriation of children are initiated.

Brazil

February   Constitutional amendment allowing for presidential reelection is approved.

June   The armed forces announce a new commemorative agenda. March 31, the date when they used to commemorate the military coup of 1964, is deleted in the new agenda.

1998
Argentina

March   Congress repeals the Full Stop and Due Obedience laws.

June   Ex-general Videla is arrested in connection with the kidnapping and appropriation of children.

September   Beginning of the hearings in the "truth trials" in the city of La Plata. These trials are geared to investigate and establish the "truth" about the fate of thousands of cases of forced disappearances but cannot end in punishment of the guilty, because of the Full Stop and Due Obedience laws.

November   Ex-Navy commander Emilio Massera is arrested in connection with the kidnapping of children during dictatorship.

Brazil

October   Fernando Henrique Cardoso is reelected president.

Chile

March   Amid massive protests, Pinochet steps down as army commander-in-chief and assumes a lifetime seat in the senate.

October Pinochet is arrested in London on a warrant issued by Spanish judge Baltazar Garzón. Legal battles over his extradition to Spain ensue.

Paraguay

Raúl Cubas Grau is elected president.

1999
Argentina

April "Truth trials" begin in Rosario.
September The Argentine government accepts the OAS declaration recognizing that the right to truth does not prescribe.
October Fernando de la Rúa is elected president.
November "Truth trials" begin in Bahia Blanca.

Brazil

March The attorney general asks the military courts to reopen the Riocentro case.

Chile

Chilean judges order several arrests of retired army officers on kidnapping charges.

Paraguay

March Vice President Luis María Argaña is assassinated amid major political conflicts. Street fighting erupts when massive street demonstrations in support of the proposal to impeach President Cubas are met by repression. President Cubas resigns, and Luis González Macchi, president of the House, is sworn in as president of the country. Ex-president Cubas flees to Brazil, and General Lino Oviedo enters Argentina illegally.

Uruguay-Argentina

October Argentine poet Juan Gelman sends an open letter to President Sanguinetti, asking him to investigate the fate of his disappeared grandchild. An international solidarity campaign ensues.

2000
Argentina

December   Ex-generals Guillermo Suárez Mason and Santiago Omar Riveros are sentenced (in absentia) to life imprisonment in Italy.

Brazil

May   The Supreme Military Tribunal (Supremo Tribunal Militar) decides one more time to close (this time for good) the Riocentro case.

Uruguay

March 1   Jorge Batlle is sworn in as president. He creates a "peace commission" as a step toward reconciliation.

March 31   President Batlle and Juan Gelman publicly announce that Gelman's abducted granddaughter has been located in Montevideo.

Chile

March   Pinochet returns to Chile after being released in Britain on medical grounds.

March   Ricardo Lagos is sworn in as president.

June   The Roundtable Dialogue (Mesa de Diálogo), convened in 1999, reaches an agreement and signs an accord. Each branch of the armed forces, including the uniformed police, agree to provide the fullest information possible on the whereabouts or fate of the "disappeared" at the end of six months.

2001
Argentina

March   Judge Gabriel Cavallo declares that the Full Stop and Due Obedience Laws are unconstitutional, a charge that is confirmed by the court of appeals in November.

March   Citizens rally in remembrance of the twenty-fifth
         anniversary of the military coup.

December In an atmosphere of economic and political crisis,
         street demonstrations and police repression bring
         about President de la Rúa's resignation. Congress
         elects an interim president, Adolfo Rodriguez Saá,
         who resigns after one week. Congress then elects
         Eduardo Duhalde as interim president.

2002
Brazil

October Luiz Ignacio da Silva (Lula) is elected president.

Chile

July   The Chilean Supreme Court decides to terminate
         the prosecution of General Augusto Pinochet.

Notes

Introduction

1. The appendix presents a very schematic chronological ordering of the most significant events in the political developments in the region during the period.

2. In the 1990s, new important actors entered the struggle for justice: third-country justice systems (in Europe and in the region itself) and international agencies and courts. The role of these actors is on the increase, creating a threefold impact: some perpetrators are being subjected to criminal and civil judgments and criminal verdicts (often in absentia), mass media attention to rights violations has generated debates in the public sphere in each country, and pressures have increased accordingly on the judiciary in the countries where the violations took place.

3. Interpretations of the past are the subject of social controversies even after centuries. This was evident in the commemorations of the five-hundred-year anniversary of Columbus's arrival in America, in 1492. Was it the "discovery" of America or its "conquest"? Was it an "encounter" of different cultures or the beginning of the "genocide" of indigenous peoples? Different actors attached different meanings and interpretations, and even different names, to what was being remembered in 1992. There was no possibility of having a single unified commemoration.

1. Memory in the Contemporary World

1. Pierre Nora (1996), a key figure in current thought and research on memory, argues that modern memory is, above all, archival. It rests entirely on the materiality of the trace, on the immediacy of the record, on the visibility of the image. See also Gillis 1994.

2. This acceleration was related to, among other things, "media attention paid to the 40th and 50th anniversaries of events that took place during the Third Reich:

Hitler's rise to power in 1933 and the infamous book burnings remembered in 1983; *Kristallnacht,* the organized pogrom of 1938 against Germany's Jews publicly commemorated in 1988; . . . the end of World War II in 1945 remembered in 1985 . . . and again in 1995 with a whole series of international events in Europe and Japan" (Huyssen 2000, 22–23).

3. The notion of "social catastrophe" is taken from René Kaës (1991), who derives it from the concept of "psychic catastrophe": "A psychic catastrophe occurs when the habitual modes of coping with the negativity inherent in a traumatic experience are insufficient, especially when they cannot be used by the subject due to specific features of the relationship between the internal traumatic reality and the environment" (142). A social catastrophe involves the "annihilation (or perversion) of the imaginary and symbolic systems inherent in social and transgenerational institutions, affecting the basic prescriptions regulating shared representations, prohibitions, structuring contracts, inter-subjective places and practices. . . . Situations of social catastrophe bring about ruptures in the psychic work of attachment, representation and articulation. . . . As Freud emphasized, while natural catastrophes promote social solidarity, social catastrophes disaggregate and divide the social body" (144–45).

4. The expression *Nunca Más* ("Never Again") has gained iconic status in the region. It is a slogan charged with emotional and instrumental meanings. Not by chance, the expression has been used as the title of the reports on human rights violations during dictatorships in Argentina, Uruguay, and Brazil (*Nunca más,* 1984; *Brasil: Nunca mais,* 1985; *Uruguay Nunca Más,* 1989). A comparative analysis of these and the Chilean report, including their iconic position in societal memories, is found in Marchesi 2002b.

5. Freud contrasts mourning to melancholy. In the latter, the loss can be imaginary, and the ego identifies with the lost object. This leads to a loss of respect for one's own self (Freud 1976, 243).

2. What Memories Are We Talking About?

1. While working on this chapter and rereading Halbwachs, I realized that he just about ignores the relationship between memory and suffering or trauma. Social memory for him is reinforced by social belonging, by the group. The individual fades in the collective. Meanwhile, I also began to read Jorge Semprún's book (1997) *La escritura o la vida* (translated into English as *Literature or Life*). And shortly I encountered Halbwachs, the individual. Semprún writes that while detained in the Buchenwald concentration camp, he found a way to break the discipline and massification of the "invisibility" of camp experience through personalized connections. He finds in Halbwachs, his Sorbonne professor who is agonizing in the camp, someone in whom he can deposit the "vestiges" of his own human condition by visiting him, speaking to him, accompanying his agony. Fifty years later, Semprún incorporates this into his "memory." The two endpoints, the individual and the collective, the personalized experience and the destitution of the human condition in the camp, converge. He reflects: "[death] was the substance of our brotherhood, the key to our destiny, the sign of our membership in the community of the living. Together we lived the experience of that death, that compassion. This defined our being: to be with one another as death advanced upon us. . . . All we who were going to die had chosen the fraternity of this death through a love of freedom. That is what I learned from the gaze of Maurice Halbwachs, as he lay dying" (24).

2. In his analysis of the meaning of Captain Cook's death in Hawaii, Marshall Sahlins (1987) shows how "Cook was a tradition for Hawaiians before he was a fact"

(148). An analogous thesis has been advanced with respect to the arrival of the Spaniards in Mexico (Todorov 1997).

3. "Memory is a constitutive element of the sense of identity, both individual or collective, insofar as it is an extremely important factor of the sense of continuity and coherence for the person or the group in the process of reconstructing itself" (Pollak 1992, 204).

4. "Recollection results from an ongoing psychic process, consisting of working through the residues of a screen memory, of a ghost or a dream, in order to construct a new arrangement between elements that represent the subject's eventful, libidinal, or identificatory past, and his current positioning vis-à-vis that past—what he can bear knowing and not knowing about it" (Enriquez 1990, 121).

5. The opening scene in *The Book of Laughter and Forgetting* reads, "In February, 1948, the Communist leader Klement Gottwald stepped out on the balcony of a Baroque palace in Prague to harangue hundreds of thousands of citizens massed in Old City Square. . . . Gottwald was flanked by his comrades, with Clementis standing close to him. It was snowing and cold, and Gottwald was bareheaded. Bursting with solicitude, Clementis took off his fur hat and set it on Gottwald's head. The propaganda section made hundreds of thousands of copies of the photograph taken on the balcony where Gottwald, in a fur and surrounded by his comrades, spoke to the people. . . . Four years later, Clementis was charged with treason and hanged. The propaganda section immediately made him vanish from history and, of course, from all photographs. Ever since, Gottwald has been alone on the balcony. Where Clementis stood, there is only the bare palace wall. Nothing remains of Clementis but the fur hat on Gottwald's head" (Kundera 1996, 3–4). Another famous political erasure of a public image is that of Trotsky accompanying Lenin.

6. Ricoeur (2000) examines the issue of forgetting in depth. The discussion that follows comes from Ricoeur 1999 (103 et seq.), which summarizes the thinking developed in his subsequent larger book (Ricoeur 2000).

7. In 2000, a case was brought to court in the United Kingdom that turned on the interpretation of the Shoah, insofar as one of the parties based its case on the fact that there has been no written order for the "final solution" signed by Hitler. The careful destruction of evidence and traces of repression in the Southern Cone of South America is well known—especially the destruction of documentation and the disappearance of the bodies of the kidnapped persons. To make the scene even more macabre, in Argentina, testimony occasionally surfaces from neighbors (and even by the perpetrators themselves) reporting the existence of clandestine detention camps that had not been denounced or registered before, since they were total annihilation camps, which meant there were no survivors. These revelations show—as is well known by writers of crime literature—that it is not easy to achieve a "perfect crime."

8. The various meanings of *repression* are appropriate here. To *repress* is "to keep under control, check or suppress (desires, feelings, actions); to keep down anything objectionable; to put down or quell disorder; to reject painful or disagreeable ideas, memories, feelings or impulses from the conscious mind" (*Random House Webster's Dictionary* 1998).

9. "1945 organizes the act of forgetting deportations. The deportees return when new ideologies are already established, when the battle for memory is already on its way, when the political scene is already set up: they are superfluous" (Namer 1983, cited in Pollak 1989, 6).

10. " . . . a memory of a memory, a memory that is possible because it evokes another memory. We can remember only thanks to the fact that somebody has remembered

before us, that other people in the past have challenged death and terror on the basis of their memory. Remembering has to be conceived as a highly inter-subjective relationship" (Passerini 1992a, 2).

3. Political Struggles for Memory

1. "Even though, in effect, events are unerasable and what is done cannot be undone, nor can what happened be made not to happen, the meaning of what happened is never fixed once and for all. Not only can the events of the past be interpreted in a different way; the moral weight linked to the debt with the past can increase or decrease, depending on whether primacy is given to the accusation, which traps the guilty in the painful feeling of irreversibility, or the pardon, which leads to condoning the debt, which is equivalent to a conversion in the meaning of the past itself. This phenomenon of reinterpretation can be considered both at the moral level and as a simple story, as a case of retroactive action of the intentions towards the future on the portrayal of the past" (Ricoeur 1999, 49).

2. For the relationship between memory and the nation, and for an analysis of specific cases, see the special issue of *Social Science History*, edited by Jeffrey Olick (1998b).

3. ". . . it is no longer merely a question of the decay of collective memory . . . but of the aggressive rape of whatever memory remains, the deliberate distortion of the historical record, the invention of mythological pasts in the service of the powers of darkness. Against the agents of oblivion, the shredders of documents, the assassins of memory, the revisers of encyclopedias, the conspirators of silence, against those who, in Kundera's wonderful image, can airbrush a man out of a photograph so that nothing is left of him but his hat—only the historian, with the austere passion for fact, proof, evidence, which are central to his vocation, can effectively stand guard" (Yerushalmi 1989, 116).

4. The persistence and appropriation of the icons of protest music and of censored slogans among young people that could not have lived through the earlier direct experience of expressing them in public spaces during the dictatorships are clear examples of this nonlinearity of memory. When Spain opened up in the late 1970s, adolescents sang Republican songs from the Civil War and chanted slogans from that era as if they were their own. In the Argentine transition, young people began publicly singing the songs of the famous singer Mercedes Sosa (whose works were censored for public performance during the military dictatorship) as if they had a long-term and direct contact with her. Pollak (1989) describes several European cases of silenced memories.

5. "Spanish society attempted . . . not to reproduce the errors that had undermined the Second Republic. The replication of its institutional design was avoided in an almost superstitious way. . . . This is one of the reasons that best explains the preference for a monarchy over a republic, for an electoral system based on proportional representation rather than on simple majority . . ." (Aguilar Fernández 1996, 360).

6. This interpretation of the Spanish transition and the role of political forgetting can be read in the code that Nicole Loraux proposed for ancient Greece: amnesty (and amnesia) in the political field as a means for constructing a new pact or a new covenant, and the reemergence of the conflict-ridden past in symbolic cultural expressions through classical tragedy. Furthermore, Loraux (1989) pays attention to a gender specificity that merits mentioning. While the political men forget the past conflicts and build institutions, the women in tragedy theater express pain and cry for their dead.

7. A chronology of the main political decisions and measures taken in the countries of the region is presented in the appendix.

8. The role of the human rights movement in the Argentine transition, both with respect to memory and to demands for justice, is analyzed in Jelin 1995. For an analysis of civil-military relations in the transitions of Argentina, Brazil, and Chile, see Acuña and Smulovitz 1996.

9. The use of the word *entrepreneur* should not be limited to its association with enterprise for private profit. As used here, it refers to entrepreneurial actions of a "social" or collective nature. The important point is that the entrepreneur becomes personally involved in his or her project; in addition, she or he generates commitment from others, fostering participation and organizing efforts of a collective character. Unlike "militants of memory" (a term used by Rousso, for example), entrepreneurs generate projects, new ideas, expressions, and creative initiatives—rather than repeating time and again the same script. The notion of entrepreneur also implies the existence of a social organization connected to the project of memory, involving social hierarchies, control mechanisms, and a division of labor under the control of the entrepreneurs.

10. Claudia Feld (2002) analyzes Argentine television and the "spectacularization" of the memories of dictatorship. When in 1998, public television broadcast a special program on the ESMA (Escuela de Mecánica de la Armada, the most important center of clandestine detention during the military dictatorship) anchored by the well-known journalist and former member of CONADEP (National Commission for the Disappeared) Magdalena Ruiz Guiñazú, newspapers reported the broadcast under the headline: "Memory has high rating."

11. Organizations of the relatives of the disappeared, murdered, and imprisoned were created at the height of repression during dictatorships. In Chile, the Asociación de Familiares has been active all these years. In Argentina, the Madres de Plaza de Mayo, the Abuelas de Plaza de Mayo, and the Familiares de Desaparecidos y Detenidos por Razones Politicas began their activities in 1976 and 1977, right after the military coup of March 1976, and have been active and growing for twenty-five years. In Uruguay, the organization of Madres y Familiares de Uruguayos Detenidos-Desaparecidos was created in 1983, unifying the work of three previously existing organizations (Asociación de Familiares de Uruguayos Desaparecidos [AFUDE], founded by Uruguayan exiles in Europe; Familiares de Uruguayos Desaparecidos en Argentina, founded in 1977; and Familiares de Desaparecidos en Uruguay, created in 1982). For further information, see http://www.derechos.org/nizkor/index.html.

12. In the introduction to his book, Ernst van Alphen (1997) writes autobiographically about the "saturation" of memory of Nazism that surrounded his childhood and adolescence in Holland in the 1960s and 1970s, and the reaction of distance and even rejection that this provoked in him and others of his generation.

13. Obviously, the meanings that different groups in Chilean society give to the date of September 11 will be changed by the overlay of commemorations of the attacks in the United States. Whether the new meanings will cover up the previous ones, and for whom, and the way the interaction and coincidence will be signified is something to be watched in the future.

14. This does not mean that there is no public conflict during commemorations of the 24th. Besides some occasional declarations of military men or some minor show of support for them, the confrontations are mostly between various actors *within* the human rights movement. Clearly, the date and the commemoration have different meanings for the diverse groups (the central rally in the city of Buenos Aires is organized by more than two hundred social organizations) and collective identities that play out in that space.

15. Analyses of these types of conflict have been the object of now classic studies

in cultural criticism. James Young (1993, 2000) has analyzed the conflicts surrounding different monuments and artworks proposed to commemorate the Nazi extermination. Lisa Yoneyama (1999) looks at the case of the Hiroshima Memorial, Edward Linenthal (1995) tells the story of the Holocaust museum in Washington, D.C., and Marita Sturken (1997) deals with the story of the Vietnam Memorial in Washington, D.C. Discussion of some physical markers in the Southern Cone can be found in Jelin and Langland 2003, Richard 2001, and the articles included in *Punto de Vista* (2000).

16. At that site, several events of public commemoration were carried out in the mid-1990s, installing physical markers such as murals, plaques with names of perpetrators, and a commemorative sculpture. On successive occasions, these images were destroyed during the night following their installation. Finally, some signs that were successfully installed have lasted and have not been vandalized (Jelin and Kaufman 2000). Once the site was publicly recognized, demands that the site be excavated to recover and preserve the ruins of the building and its function were successful, and the government of the city of Buenos Aires has taken the responsibility for this urban archaeology project.

17. The lack of materialization becomes critical when it involves memories of the disappeared, since the absence of bodies and the uncertainty of death make mourning almost impossible. Subjectively, to have a material marker or a place seems to help in that process of difficult mourning.

18. Rousso argues that the problem is not militancy in itself but the danger when ends are seen as justifying means, when the militants "are willing to lie about history, often purposefully, in order to safeguard a pure and simple idea about the past, with the 'good' and the 'bad' characters well identified, regardless of the complexities of human behavior" (in Feld 2000, 37). See also Rousso 2002.

19. I learned of this distinction from Line Bareiro, a Paraguayan colleague who shares my interest in these issues. The Guaraní words are not accented, since in that language all words that end in a vowel are stressed on the last syllable.

20. The symbols of personal suffering tend to be embodied in women—the mothers and grandmothers in the case of Argentina—while the institutional mechanisms seem to belong more often to the world of men. The significance of this gender dimension and the difficulties of breaking gender stereotypes with respect to the resources of power call for much more analytical attention. Future research should also study the impact that the prevailing image—in the human rights movement and society as a whole—of demands for *Truth* based on suffering and on images of family and family relationships has on the process of building a culture of citizenship and equality (Filc 1997). Ludmila da Silva Catela (2001) also discusses these issues.

4. History and Social Memory

1. An exhaustive review of the literature on this topic is beyond the scope and objective of this chapter. The relationship between history and memory is at the heart of current disciplinary debates in the field of history, beginning with the works of Pierre Nora (1984–92); see also LaCapra 1998.

2. The normalizing and structuring role played by the researcher (in the broadest sense, as someone who investigates or asks questions) is present in all social interactions. The clearest institutionalized manifestation of the power differentials between interrogating and narrating subjects is the police interrogation, although these are also present and influential in the relationship established by a journalist in an interview, in a research interview, or in the therapeutic relationship between analyst and patient.

3. LaCapra provides an in-depth analysis of these issues, searching for a mode of

writing and narrating that can overcome the oppositions between radical positivism and radical constructivism (between objectivity and subjectivity, cognition and affect, reconstruction and dialogue, and so on) and that can allow for the articulation of relationships in a more reflexive and self-critical fashion. This search leads him to Roland Barthes's "middle voice," a voice that "requires modulations of proximity and distance, empathy and irony with respect to the different 'objects' of investigation" (LaCapra 2001, 30).

4. In January 1999, a group of Chilean historians published their *Manifiesto de historiadores* in response to a *Carta a los chilenos* that Pinochet published, from his detention place in London. The historians denounced the manipulation of facts involved in that *Carta* and presented their understanding of the past fifty years of Chilean history. They did so from the perspective of the discipline of history and from their position as citizens committed to the defense of human rights. The *Manifiesto* produced widespread public support and controversy (Grez and Salazar 1999).

5. The terminology used to name what has taken place is part of the struggle over the meanings of the past. The ways of naming can also acquire different meanings that change over time. In relation to the events in Europe during the Nazi period, and specifically the genocide committed against Jews, there is an implicit debate about the use of the word *Holocaust,* which etymologically has connotations of religious sacrifice and ritual purification. I prefer to use the more neutral expression "Nazi extermination," or the Hebrew word *Shoah,* in its sense of catastrophe or devastation (both natural and human), to avoid entering this debate about the implicit meaning in the act of naming, recognizing at the same time the sinister character of the historical event. Giorgio Agamben (2000, 25–31) dedicates several pages of very lucid writing to the etymology of these words and their implication in the process of naming, which explain his decision not to use the term *Holocaust*. LaCapra (2001), on the other hand, shows how, as the use of this term has become generalized, its original etymological meaning and its connotation of ritual sacrifice have been completely lost.

6. In the context of the trial, for example, almost all questions that alluded to the ideological or political affiliations of the witness—many of whom were survivors of clandestine detention centers who were narrating their experiences of torture and degradation—were struck down by the judges. Only on a few occasions, and with the explicit objective of demonstrating the systematic nature of the armed forces' plan of extermination, did the judges allow questions of this nature (Acuña and Smulovitz 1995; González Bombal 1995).

7. An analysis of the "truth trials" conducted in a number of Argentine jurisdictions starting in 1995 may be helpful in revealing the continuity or change in this depoliticized interpretation of the past. In fact, these new trials do not hide the political conflicts of the 1970s or the political agency of the victims. At this point, it is also appropriate to raise a comparative question: What kind of victim figure was constructed in countries where there were no trials? In Brazil, for example, the political activism of militants was never silenced and served as a strong referent in the construction of the figure of the victims of repression in that country. On the other hand, the Brazilian military also made their vision and their voices heard in a very public and powerful manner and participated actively in the construction of the narratives about the military regime in that country (Soares and D'Araujo 1994; Soares, D'Araujo, and Castro 1995; Castro and D'Araujo 2001).

8. The political circumstances in the Southern Cone beginning in 2000 offer a clear example of this, as has already been mentioned. Any observer of the political situation in these countries in the early 1990s could easily have come to the conclusion that a

kind of "state of equilibrium" had been reached, and although it may have been unsatisfactory to many, it at least permitted a minimal level of "peaceful coexistence." The presidential pardons of the convicted members of the military in Argentina, a negotiated transition in Chile, the plebiscite in Uruguay that led to accepting amnesty for past violations of human rights, direct presidential elections in Brazil, and the defeat of the guerrilla movement Sendero Luminoso in Peru were all indicators of a certain degree of "social calm," in which institutional practices appeared to be achieving a minimum level of routinization. Ten years later, the scenarios were in total convulsion. Pinochet's detention in London initiated a new wave of demands and judicial procedures in Chile; in Uruguay a Commission for Peace was created, and the government recognized that there had been a state policy of human rights violations in the past; there have been attempts to reopen cases against the Brazilian state for its role in repression and continuing demands for reparations on the part of victims; and there are ongoing truth trials and new cases brought to the courts regarding the kidnapping of children in Argentina. (There was a historic court decision in 2001 declaring the Final Stop and Due Obedience Laws unconstitutional, and in 2002 the issue is on the agenda of the Supreme Court). In all countries, the demand for discovering and opening up of archives of repression is increasingly active (da Silva Catela and Jelin 2002).

9. On this point, Portelli argues that the Italian Left failed in its attempt to incorporate civilian victims of the resistance into its historical narrative. To do so, they would have had to explicitly recognize the resistance as *war*, and not as a morally based movement of all Italians. With this failure, Portelli contends, the Italian Left made a very costly contribution to its own defeat in the struggle over memory (Portelli 1999; 1997, chap. 10).

5. Trauma, Testimony, and "Truth"

1. Silence, as opposed to oblivion, may function as a means of coping with issues related to managing identity reconstruction, resulting from the work involved in trying to reinsert oneself in the world of "normal" life. Silence can also express the difficulty of making the testimonial narrative coincide with dominant moral strictures, or the absence of favorable social conditions that would authorize, solicit, or open the possibility of listening (Pollak 1990; Pollak and Heinich 1986).

2. In the language of Auschwitz, the *Muselmann* was the prisoner who had abandoned the hope and the will to live, "a walking corpse, a bundle of physiological functions already in agony," as J. Amery describes it (cited in Agamben 1999, 41). This is the limit situation between the human and the nonhuman, in the conceptualization of Agamben (1999).

3. Laub (1992a, 76) makes reference to his own extremely precise memory (as a child who survived), including an understanding of what was taking place, in a way that was "far beyond the normal capacity for recall in a young child of my age." He also finds this feature of a "precocious memory" among other survivors that he interviewed.

4. Wieviorka (1998) refers to the enormous number of documents and testimonials written by Jews in the ghettos and the camps at the time the atrocities were taking place. They responded to an imperative to record and record, and also served as a form of resistance in the face of extermination: "Good people, do not forget, good people, tell the story, good people, write!" exclaimed historian Simon Dobnov before his death during the destruction of the ghetto in Riga in 1941 (Wieviorka 1999, 125). There is little doubt that large numbers of these writings, which had been hidden in bottles and walls, were lost to Nazi hands. Yet some survived.

5. Once again, as in previous chapters, we encounter evidence that the temporality

of memories is not linear but is instead characterized by fractures, gaps, and lapses. Just as the "feverish" search to find systematic ways to preserve the testimonials of Shoah survivors took place several decades after the event (first with the Fortunoff Audiovisual Testimonial Archive at Yale and with the Yad Vashem Museum in Jerusalem; more recently with the project to collect survivors' testimonies sponsored by S. Spielberg), the era of systematic testimonials is just now arriving in the Southern Cone. There is the Oral History Archive, for example, which is being developed by the organization Memoria Abierta in Argentina (http://www.memoriaabierta.org.ar).

6. "If the experience of the camps lies at the limits of all human experience, testimonial experiences are no less extreme. . . . The request to narrate humiliating memories and the difficulties involved in doing so can easily generate a feeling of obligation to give testimony, but also a need to justify one's relationship to the events that are narrated. This, in turn, can lead to a feeling of being the accused rather than the witness . . ." (Pollak 1990, 186).

7. "Not to understand was my iron law during all the eleven years of the production of *Shoah*. I clung to this refusal of understanding as the only possible ethical and at the same time the only possible operative attitude. This blindness was for me the vital condition of creation. Blindness has to be understood here as the purest mode of looking, of the gaze, the only way to not turn away from a reality which is literally blinding . . ." (Lanzmann 1995, 204).

8. For example, as a result of the "mistake" of a survivor about the number of chimneys in Auschwitz, the full veracity of the testimony became a topic of contention between interviewers and historians, as Laub (1992a) points out.

9. The issue of "truth" and its lack of correlation with the credibility of a testimonial are clearly brought to the fore in the history of the reception of *Yosl Rakover Speaks to God* (Kolitz 1999). In this case, readers wanted to believe that the story was true despite the repeated statements to the contrary by the author, who insisted that his text was fiction written in the first person and not the testimony of a witness as is suggested in the initial pages of the text: "In one of the ruins of the Warsaw ghetto, preserved in a little bottle and concealed amongst heaps of charred stone and human bones, the following testament was found, written in the last hours of the ghetto by a Jew named Yosl Rakover" (3).

10. If, as Semprún so vividly conveys, the concentration camp is lived through as death, the life experience that follows comes into conflict with the available interpretive frameworks of the life course, because the passing of time distances the subject from his or her own death. This contradicts the "normal" idea of the life course, where to the extent that time passes, death becomes closer. Much time has to elapse and much capacity to symbolize has to be learned to convey the testimony. Semprún wrote his testimony about life in Buchenwald fifty years after his being there. He states that he did not do it earlier because "between writing and living," he chose the latter (1997). As was pointed out earlier, Semprún's posture is not the only one possible. There are other ways in which survivors have negotiated their identities and their ability to give testimony.

11. The parallel with the early stages of feminism, when the task of "making visible the invisible" combined research, denunciation, and demands, is not coincidental. Many testimonies have been of women, and many of the mediators have been part of the feminist movement.

12. When analyzing the personal narratives of World War I combatants, Samuel Hynes (1999) makes the opposite point, arguing that "each example tells the story of one man in actions involving many, and that each speaks in its own individual voice, which is not the voice of history, nor of collective memory" (218–19). The author also argues that the very existence of these individual narratives "refutes and subverts

the collective narrative of the war, which is the narrative of military history" (220). Annette Wieviorka, for her part, warns of a clear danger that emerges in the "era of the testimonial"—the danger of the fragmentation of historical and collective narrative into a series of individual histories. In this context, the Shoah can lose its political character and come to be perceived only as the cause of the devastation of individual lives, which results in the transformation of political categories into categories of individual psychology (Wieviorka 1999, 140).

13. Operation Condor was a systematic plan to coordinate repression between the armed forces of Chile, Argentina, Uruguay, Brazil, Paraguay, and Bolivia. Although information about its practices did exist due to the testimony of victims and witnesses such as Lilian Celiberti herself, the existence of the plan was confirmed by the discovery and analysis of the archives of the Paraguayan Secret Police in 1992, the subsequent declassification of documents about the case by the U.S. State Department in 1999, and the opening of the archives of the Brazilian Secret Police (Boccia Paz 1999; Boccia Paz et al. 2002).

14. In the case being analyzed, Lilian Celiberti asked Lucy Garrido to help in the construction of her narrative, built in an interview format.

15. In their work on political violence in the Ayacucho region of Peru, Ponciano del Pino (2003) and del Pino and Kimberly Theidon (1999) show how the memories of peasants are constructed at the intersection between their indigenous worldviews and recently introduced evangelical religions, which offer a new framework to interpret and give some sense to the violence of the recent past. See also the papers included in Stern 1998.

6. Engendered Memories

1. This section is based on an essay by Teresa Valdés, "Algunas ideas para la consideración de la dimensión de género en la memoria colectiva de la represión," document prepared for the Social Science Research Council Memory Program, 1999.

2. In a highly schematic way, a gender system involves: (a) a dominant sexual division of labor (production/reproduction); (b) a differentiation of social spheres and spaces based on gender (a visible public sphere/an invisible private sphere); (c) differential power relations and hierarchical distinctions, involving different quotas of recognition, prestige, and legitimacy; (d) power relations within each gender (based on class, ethnicity, etc.); (e) the construction of gender identities that coincide with other vectors of difference, producing a masculine identity anchored in work, the role of "provider," and the administration of power, and a feminine identity anchored in domestic work, maternity, and the social role of "the wife"; (f) the construction of "dominant" identities associated with the power relations in society (hetero/homosexuals, white/black-indigenous-poor).

3. Diana Taylor (1997) examines this gender performance in the actions of the military junta in Argentina, and demonstrates how women, within these contexts, become "un-representable" as subjects, so that representation becomes, by definition, a masculine self-representation.

4. These practices are not exclusive to militaries from the Southern Cone. According to Theweteit, the construction of Nazi masculinity consisted of "a cultivation of both sadistic aggression and masochistic discipline and self-sacrifice" (cited by van Alphen 1997, 58).

5. Bunster points out that the most horrific situation was when women were kidnapped from their homes. "The arrest of a woman in her home, in front of her children,

is doubly painful for Latin American women. Tradition makes her the foundation of the family . . ." (Bunster 1991, 48).

6. The active role in sexual intercourse between men, which was what torturers did, was not identified with homosexuality or with being "feminized." It was specifically the passive role that was identified as feminine (Salessi 1995; Taylor 1997).

7. The case of a young female student who by befriending the daughter of a police chief was able to put a bomb under his bed is a paradigmatic example. "Then, on one tragic night, a teen-ager, Ana María González, sneaks into 'the friendliest of homes' and, betraying all sentiments of friendship, gratitude and honor, she carries out in COLD BLOOD the mission of assassinating a man. It did not matter that the man was a National General. It did not matter that he was the chief of the Federal Police. HE WAS A MAN who when going to bed was going to face his last sleep, killed by an explosive device set by his daughter's best friend." This is how the event was described by the renowned journalist B. Neustadt in a popular Argentine magazine (Bernardo Neustadt, "¿Se preguntó cuántas Anas Marías González hay?" Revista *Gente*, Year 11, N° 571, July 11, 1976, 76).

8. These aspects of the organization of everyday life in the face of the kidnapping and disappearance of their partners are clearly portrayed in the testimonies collected by Ciollaro (2000). They are also present from the perspective of the children in some of the testimonies gathered by Gelman and La Madrid (1997).

9. The dictatorships, moreover, sought to discipline everyday life not only through repression but also through specific public policies. In Chile, policies designed to "protect" women and to "support" their role as the foundation of the social model proposed by the regime CEMA-Chile and the National Secretariat for Women were clear examples of such policies. At this point, it is useful to remember that an active policy regarding women and the family was also a central feature of the Nazi regime. Although the emphasis was on promoting women to devote themselves only to "the three K's," *Kirche, Kuche, Kinder* (church, kitchen, children), there was widespread mobilization of women in public organizations devoted to implementing policies designed to encourage women to fulfill their traditional roles (Koonz 1988).

10. On this point, cognitive studies indicate that "in general terms" neither men nor women have a "better" memory. This makes it necessary to explore differences linked to specific kinds or modalities of memory (spatial versus temporal, episodic or semantic, memory of lived experience versus transmitted memory, etc.) (see Loftus et al. 1987, for example). There has not been much research of this kind, particularly research that looks at situations with high degrees of emotional involvement. Gender is not a significant variable in studies devoted to present current research results and explanations of memory (Schacter 1996, 2001).

11. Pollak (1990) establishes these distinctions in his analysis of the narratives of female Auschwitz survivors. In a subtle reading, he shows the diversity of discursive strategies: chronological or thematic, personal or political, centered exclusively on concentration camp experience or including narratives of the "before" and "after," and so on. He also demonstrates the importance of the historical moment and the social circumstances in which the memories of deportation are evoked (immediately after the war, years afterwards, as a response to institutional demands, or as a personal decision to transmit the experience) to their elaboration in these diverse contexts. His analysis of this body of testimonials, however, does not include a comparison with the testimonies of men or an analysis of the gender relations present in the production of these narratives.

12. The annihilation of women as bearers of specific ethno-racial identities took on

a different character in the former Yugoslavia—rape was the means of "ethnic cleansing" (Mostov 2000).

13. The political controversy involves debates about the responsibility of the Japanese state, demands for economic reparations, and highly charged debates about whether to include these events in school textbooks. Throughout this controversy, political debate has been presented (or perhaps masked) as a scholarly historical debate about "what actually happened," given the absence of written documents and the fact that existing evidence consists mostly of testimonials (Sand 1999).

14. At the end of the war, many of these women were executed or abandoned. Most of them died. Among the survivors, very few returned to their places of origin, shameful of their ill repute and certain that they would be rejected by their families. The few that married and had children never mentioned their "shameful" past, not even to their closest relatives. "Japanese aggression had succeeded in muting its victims" (Chizuko 1999, 131).

15. This history included debates about whether the issue involved slavery or prostitution, and whether this bureaucratic organization of sexual services was "preferable" or "more benevolent" than private brothels.

16. Here we refer to public testimonies and narratives. Therapeutic processes with patients who lived through extreme or limit conditions (clandestine detention centers, torture) belong to a different level of analysis. Amati Sas (1991) lays out the dilemmas and specific conditions of these therapeutic situations and shows the role played by emotions, particularly the "recuperation of shame," in the therapeutic process.

17. Interestingly enough, women predominate not only in narrating the pains and suffering of repression but also in the academic and intellectual community of scholars interested in these subjects. Gendered sensibilities undoubtedly are present, yet the issue calls for further attention.

7. Transmissions, Legacies, Lessons

1. This is not to imply the absence of transmission of meanings, but rather that what was conveyed were not necessarily the meanings intended by the older generations. As numerous studies on the subject indicate, intergenerational transmission does not take place exclusively through explicitly verbal channels but also through silences, through lapses and fears. Helen Epstein (1988) refers to the children of the survivors as "a group of people who, like me, were possessed by a history they had never lived" (14).

2. H.I.J.O.S (Hijos por la Identidad y la Justicia contra el Olvido y el Silencio [Children for Identity and Justice and against Oblivion and Silence]) is an organization that emerged during the 1990s. Initially it grouped children of the disappeared in Argentina, and over time its membership broadened to encompass other young people who have had repressive experiences or identify with their views. Its strategies of public action are innovative and different from those employed by the rest of the country's human rights organizations, including *escraches* (public shaming of repressors). The organization has also expanded to other Southern Cone countries and to exiled communities all over the world. For a critical view of the political implications of the *escraches*, see Vezzetti 1998.

3. In his monumental work on "realms of memory" *(Les lieux de mémoire)* in France, Pierre Nora includes the notion of "generation" as a realm of memory and comes to the conclusion that it is possible to speak of French generations. These emerge when, besides sharing both experiences and memories, actors become witnesses of their own action (in other words, through reflexivity), and new witnesses, in turn, become actors. The presence of these three elements is what feeds the generational "blaze."

"The play goes on, and it is up to each generation to rewrite its generational history" (Nora 1996, 531).

4. Van Alphen (1997) juxtaposes the notions of "Holocaust representation" and "Holocaust effect," and leans toward the latter. He argues that "a representation is, by definition, mediated. It is an objectified account. The Holocaust is made present in the representation of it by means of *reference* to it. When I call something a Holocaust effect, . . . we, as viewers or readers, experience directly a certain aspect of the Holocaust or of Nazism, of that which led to the Holocaust. In such moments the Holocaust is not re-presented, but rather presented or reenacted. . . . It is made present as performative effect. Those performative acts 'do' the Holocaust, or rather, they 'do' a specific aspect of it" (10).

5. The weight of the past, according to Paloma Aguilar Fernández (1996), can become excessive. "One tends to see one's contemporary adversaries through the prism of the adversary that one had in the past"; "the probabilities of erroneously perceiving present problems increase when an actor had directly experienced similar situations in the past" (52).

6. Although at first sight this formulation may seem overly mechanical, its explanatory power is significant. Besides her analysis of the Spanish transition in terms of the lessons and oblivions involved in such generational succession, Luisa Passerini's work (1996) on fascist youth is also based on a model of generational succession.

7. Clinical psychoanalysis very often operates on the basis of pathogenic identifications, including the "generational telescoping," a process of identification that "condenses a history that at least in part does not belong to the generation of the patient" (Faimberg 1996, 82). The therapeutical work of dis-identification "allows for the restitution of history insofar as it belongs to the past. In consequence, dis-identification is the condition for the liberation of desire and for the constitution of the future" (86).

8. There is a clear parallel of this case with the German controversies about the absence of documentary evidence demonstrating that Hitler ordered the planning and implementation of the "final solution." The insistence of the political Right that only written orders constitute evidence of responsibility can also be seen in other places, like Chile in the context of the accusation against Pinochet for the "Death Caravan of 1973."

9. Let us remember here that the debates about how to name particular events—whether as military "coup," "revolution," "state terrorism," or "dirty war"—are themselves part of the struggles over memory and the meanings of the past.

10. How is it that thirty years later the author writes a book about the Holocaust? "Whereas the education I received failed to make the Holocaust a meaningful event for me, Holocaust art and literature finally succeeded in calling my attention to this apocalyptic moment in human history" (van Alphen 1997, 3).

11. The issue can also lead to questions about the characteristics of the "vehicles" or cultural memory products. In reference to an Anselm Kiefer painting, van Alphen (1997) shows that a work of art can document, analyze, work through, reenact, or directly reveal the past, without the mediation of a narrator (chap. 1).

12. *"The years go by, and my dad still hasn't lost that fear. Yesterday there was a student demonstration in the Plaza de Mayo, and my husband was one of the security monitors . . . And his face appeared in the TV news. Well, my father had a fit! He called, and since we were not at home he left a message on the answering machine: 'How can you do these things? You have to be more careful! It won't be long before you find yourself involved.' It's as if he extracts this image and transports it into the past. Or something*

like that, right? in other words, the fear is still here" (Julia, a young Argentine woman who lives in Buenos Aires; excerpted from Jelin and Kaufman 2000).

13. This is the tone that has characterized the contributions of various authors to a book commemorating the thirty years of 1968 in Brazil, Germany, and France. Irene Cardoso (1999), in her text on Brazil, asks about "what remained" of '68, and points to diverse modes of forgetting (on the part of the dictatorship and the Left) and to the necessity of critically scrutinizing its legacies in order to recuperate both the creative and destructive aspects of the experience. Jean-Claude Guillebaud, for his part, argues that the legacy of '68 in France is the spirit of critical inquiry and the spirit of rejection. The date is commemorated by the participants of '68, who are each time older, generating little interest among the young, who see symptoms of the *"ancien combatant"* syndrome in their commemorations (Guillebaud 1999). Peter-Erwin Jansen (1999) points out that his generation (post-'68) knew very well what '68 was all about and the ideas of the protagonists. Its critical spirit led it to oppose—not to forget—the ideas of the previous generation. This is not oblivion but reinterpretation. The author concludes that "one of our advantages was the disillusion that we inherited from '68. Whenever I listen to one of the 68ers (and in much of my life I have to listen to them), I sense that the myths grow larger each time they are told" (196).

Conclusion

1. In 1992, on the occasion of the commemoration of the fiftieth anniversary of the concentration of Jews in the Vélodrome d'Hiver in Paris for their deportation to Nazi concentration camps (in 1942), there was considerable debate about the inscription that was going to be engraved on the plaque, involving up to François Mitterand, then president of France. Finally, the plaque refers to the Vichy as the "de facto authority called 'the Government of the French State'" (Conan and Rousso 1994; Booth 1999).

Works Cited

Acuña, Carlos, and Catalina Smulovitz. 1995. "Militares en la transición argentina: del gobierno a la subordinación constitucional." In *Juicio, castigos y memorias: derechos humanos y justicia en la política argentina,* edited by Carlos Acuña et al. Buenos Aires: Nueva Visión.

———. 1996. "Adjusting the Armed Forces to Democracy: Successes, Failures, and Ambiguities in the Southern Cone." In *Constructing Democracy: Human Rights, Citizenship, and Society in Latin America,* edited by Elizabeth Jelin and Eric Hershberg. Boulder, Colo.: Westview Press.

Agamben, Giorgio. 1999. *Remnants of Auschwitz: The Witness and the Archive.* New York: Zone Books.

Aguilar Fernández, Paloma. 1996. *Memoria y olvido de la Guerra Civil Española.* Madrid: Alianza.

Amati Sas, Silvia. 1991. "Recuperar la vergüenza." In *Violencia de estado y psicoanálisis,* edited by Janine Puget and René Kaës. Buenos Aires: Centro Editor de América Latina.

Arias, Arturo, ed. 2001. *The Rigoberta Menchú Controversy.* Minneapolis: University of Minnesota Press.

Arquidiocese de Sao Paulo. 1985. *Brasil: Nunca mais.* Petrópolis: Vozes.

Bal, Mieke. 1999. Introduction to *Acts of Memory: Cultural Recall in the Present,* edited by Mieke Bal, Jonathan Crewe, and Leo Spitzer. Hanover, N.H.: University Press of New England.

Becker, Howard S. 1963. *Outsiders: Studies in the Sociology of Deviance.* New York: The Free Press.

Boccia Paz, Alfredo. 1999. "'Operativo Cóndor': ¿un ancestro vergonzoso?" *Cuadernos para el Debate,* number 7. Buenos Aires: IDES.

Boccia Paz, Alfredo, Miguel H. López, Antonio V. Pecci, and Gloria Jiménez Guanes.

2002. *En los sótanos de los generales. Los documentos ocultos del Operativo Cóndor.* Asunción: Expolibro.

Booth, James W. 1999. "Communities of Memory: On Identity, Memory, and Debt." *American Political Science Review* 93, 2.

Bourdieu, Pierre. 1985. *¿Qué significa hablar? Economía de los intercambios lingüísticos.* Madrid: Akal.

Brison, Susan J. 2002. *Aftermath: Violence and the Remaking of the Self.* Princeton, N.J.: Princeton University Press.

Bunster, Ximena. 1991. "Sobreviviendo más allá del miedo." In *La mujer ausente. Derechos humanos en el mundo,* number 15. Santiago: Isis Internacional.

Calveiro, Pilar. 1998. *Poder y desaparición. Los campos de concentración en Argentina.* Buenos Aires: Colihue.

Candina Palomer, Azun. 2002. "El día interminable. Memoria e instalación del 11 de septiembre de 1973 en Chile. 1974–1999." In *Las conmemoraciones: Las disputas en las fechas "in-felices,"* edited by Elizabeth Jelin. Madrid and Buenos Aires: Siglo XXI de España Editores/Siglo XXI de Argentina Editores.

Cardoso, Irene. 1999. "Há uma herança de 1968 no Brasil?" In *Rebeldes e contestadores. 1968. Brasil, França e Alemanha,* edited by Marco A. García and Maria A. Vieira. Sao Paulo: Fundaçao Perseu Abramo.

Caruth, Cathy. 1995. Introduction to *Trauma: Explorations in Memory.* Baltimore: The Johns Hopkins University Press.

Carvalho, Alessandra, and Ludmila da Silva Catela. 2002. "31 de marzo de 1964 en Brasil: memorias deshilachadas." In *Las conmemoraciones: Las disputas en las fechas "in-felices."* Edited by Elizabeth Jelin. Madrid and Buenos Aires: Siglo XXI de España Editores/Siglo XXI de Argentina Editores.

Castro, Celso, and María Celina D'Araujo, eds. 2001. *Militares e política na nova República.* Río de Janeiro: FGV.

Celiberti, Lilian, and Lucy Garrido. 1989. *Mi habitación, mi celda.* Montevideo: Arca.

Chizuko, Ueno. 1999. "The Politics of Memory: Nation, Individuals and Self." *History and Memory: Studies in Representation of the Past* 11, 2.

Ciollaro, Noemí. 2000. *Pájaros sin luz. Testimonios de mujeres de desaparecidos.* Buenos Aires: Planeta.

Comisión Nacional sobre la Desaparición de Personas. 1987. *Nunca más. Informe de la Comisión Nacional sobre la Desaparición de Personas.* Buenos Aires: EUDEBA.

Conan, Eric, and Henry Rousso. 1994. *Vichy, un passé qui ne passe pas.* Paris: Fayard.

Coser, Lewis A. 1992. Introduction to *On Collective Memory,* by Maurice Halbwachs. Chicago: University of Chicago Press.

da Silva Catela, Ludmila. 2001. *No habrá flores en la tumba del pasado. La experiencia de reconstrucción del mundo de los familiares de desaparecidos.* La Plata: Ediciones Al Margen.

———. 2002. "Territorios de memoria política. Los archivos de la represión en Brasil." In *Los archivos de la represión: Documentos, memoria y verdad,* edited by Ludmila da Silva Catela and Elizabeth Jelin. Madrid and Buenos Aires: Siglo XXI de España Editores/Siglo XXI de Argentina Editores.

da Silva Catela, Ludmila, and Elizabeth Jelin, eds. 2002. *Los archivos de la represión: Documentos, memoria y verdad.* Madrid and Buenos Aires: Siglo XXI de España Editores/Siglo XXI de Argentina Editores.

del Pino, Ponciano. 2003. "Uchuraccay: memoria y representación de la violencia política en los Andes." In *Luchas locales, comunidades e identidades,* edited by

Elizabeth Jelin and Ponciano del Pino. Madrid and Buenos Aires: Siglo XXI de España Editores/Siglo XXI de Argentina Editores.

del Pino, Ponciano, and Kimberly Theidon. 1999. "'Así es como vive gente': procesos deslocalizados y culturas emergentes." In *Cultura y globalización,* edited by Iván Degregori and Gonzalo Portocarrero. Lima: Red para el Desarrollo de las Ciencias Sociales en el Perú.

Diana, Marta. 1996. *Mujeres guerrilleras. La militancia de los setenta en el testimonio de sus protagonistas femeninas.* Buenos Aires: Planeta.

Dove, Patrick. 2000. "Narrations of Justice and Mourning: Testimonio and Literature in the Wake of State Terrorism in the Southern Cone." Unpublished manuscript.

Enriquez, Micheline. 1990. "La envoltura de memoria y sus huecos." In *Las envolturas psíquicas,* edited by Didier Anzier. Buenos Aires: Amorrortu.

Epstein, Helen. 1988. *Children of the Holocaust.* New York: Penguin Books.

Faimberg, Haydée. 1996. "El telescopaje [encaje] de las generaciones (Acerca de la genealogía de ciertas identificaciones)." In *Transmisión de la vida psíquica entre generaciones,* by René Kaës et al. Buenos Aires: Amorrortu.

Feld, Claudia. 2000. "Entrevista con Henry Rousso. El duelo es imposible y necesario." *Puentes* 1, 2.

———. 2002. *Del estrado a la pantalla: Las imágenes del juicio a los ex comandantes en Argentina.* Madrid and Buenos Aires: Siglo XXI de España Editores/Siglo XXI de Argentina Editores.

Filc, Judith. 1997. *Entre el parentesco y la política. Familia y dictadura, 1976–1983.* Buenos Aires: Biblos.

Franco, Jean. 1992. "Gender, Death and Resistance: Facing the Ethical Vacuum." In *Fear at the Edge: State Terror and Resistance in Latin America,* edited by Juan Corradi, Patricia Weiss Fagen, and Manuel Garretón. Berkeley: University of California Press.

———. 2002. *The Decline and Fall of the Lettered City: Latin America in the Cold War.* Cambridge and London: Harvard University Press.

Freud, Sigmund. 1976. *Duelo y melancolía,* In *Obras completas, Tomo XIV.* Buenos Aires: Amorrortu.

García Castro, Antonia. 2000. "Por un análisis político de la desaparición forzada." In *Políticas y estéticas de la memoria,* edited by Richard Nelly. Santiago: Editorial Cuarto Propio.

———. 2001. "¿Quiénes son? Los desaparecidos en la trama política chilena. 1973–2000." In *La imposibilidad del olvido. Recorridos de la memoria en Argentina, Chile y Uruguay,* edited by Bruno Groppo and Patricia Flier. La Plata: Ediciones al Margen.

Gelman, Juan, and Mara La Madrid. 1997. *Ni el flaco perdón de Dios. Hijos de desaparecidos.* Buenos Aires: Planeta.

Gillis, John R. 1994. "Memory and Identity: The History of a Relationship." In *Commemorations: The Politics of National Identity,* edited by John R. Gillis. Princeton, N.J.: Princeton University Press.

Glanz, Margo. 2001. "Harapos y tatuajes." *Mora. Revista del Instituto Interdisciplinario de Estudios de Género* 7.

Goldenberg, Myrna. 1990. "Different Horrors, Same Hell: Women Remembering the Holocaust." In *Thinking the Unthinkable: Meaning of the Holocaust,* edited by Roger Gottlieb. New York: Paulist Press.

González Bombal, María Inés. 1991. "El diálogo político: La transición que no fue." *Documento CEDES,* Number 61. Buenos Aires: CEDES.

———. 1992. "1983. El entusiasmo democrático." *Documento CEDES.* Buenos Aires: CEDES.

———. 1995. "'Nunca más'. El juicio más allá de los estrados." In *Juicio, castigos y memorias: derechos humanos y justicia en la política argentina,* by Carlos Acuña et al. Buenos Aires: Nueva Visión.

Grez, Sergio, and Gabriel Salazar, eds. 1999. *Manifiesto de historiadores.* Santiago: Lom Ediciones.

Gugelberger, Georg M. 1996a. "Introduction: Institutionalization of Transgression." In *The Real Thing,* edited by Georg M. Gugelberger. Durham, N.C.: Duke University Press.

———, ed. 1996b. *The Real Thing.* Durham, N.C.: Duke University Press.

Guillebaud, Jean-Claude. 1999. "A consolação da revolução sexual." In *Rebeldes e contestadores. 1968. Brasil, França e Alemanha,* edited by Marco A. García and Maria A. Vieira. Sao Paulo: Fundação Perseu Abramo.

Halbwachs, Maurice. 1992. *On Collective Memory.* Chicago: University of Chicago Press.

———. 1994. *Les Cadres sociaux de la mémoire.* Paris: Albin Michel.

———. 1997. *La Mémoire collective.* Paris: Albin Michel.

Hassoun, Jacques. 1996. *Los contrabandistas de la memoria.* Buenos Aires: Ediciones de la Flor.

Heimannsberg, Barbara, and Christoph J. Schmidt, eds. 1993. *The Collective Silence: German Identity and the Legacy of Shame.* San Francisco: Jossey-Bass Publishers.

Huyssen, Andreas. 2000. "Present Pasts: Media, Politics, Amnesia." *Public Culture* 12, 1.

Hynes, Samuel. 1999. "Personal Narratives and Commemoration." In *War and Remembrance in the Twentieth Century,* edited by Jay Winter and Emmanuel Sivan. Cambridge: Cambridge University Press.

Jansen, Peter-Erwin. 1999. "Heranças de 1968." In *Rebeldes e contestadores. 1968. Brasil, França e Alemanha,* edited by Marco A. García and Maria A. Vieira. Sao Paulo: Fundação Perseu Abramo.

Jelin, Elizabeth. 1995. "La política de la memoria: el movimiento de derechos humanos y la construcción democrática en la Argentina." In *Juicio, castigos y memorias: derechos humanos y justicia en la política argentina,* by Carlos Acuña et al. Buenos Aires: Nueva Visión.

———, ed. 2002a. *Las conmemoraciones: Las disputas en las fechas "in-felices."* Madrid and Buenos Aires: Siglo XXI de España Editores/Siglo XXI de Argentina Editores.

———. 2002b. "Los sentidos de la conmemoración." In *Las conmemoraciones: Las disputas en las fechas "in-felices,"* edited by Elizabeth Jelin. Madrid and Buenos Aires: Siglo XXI de España Editores/Siglo XXI de Argentina Editores.

Jelin, Elizabeth, and Susana Kaufman. 2000. "Layers of Memories: Twenty Years After in Argentina." In *The Politics of War Memory and Commemoration,* edited by T. Ashplant, Graham Dawson, and Michael Roper. London: Routledge.

Jelin, Elizabeth, and Victoria Langland. 2003. *Monumentos, memoriales y marcas territoriales.* Madrid and Buenos Aires: Siglo XXI de España Editores/Siglo XXI de Argentina Editores.

Kaës, René. 1991. "Rupturas catastróficas y trabajo de la memoria. Notas para una investigación." In *Violencia de estado y psicoanálisis,* edited by Janine Puget and René Kaës. Buenos Aires: Centro Editor de América Latina.

———. 1996. "Introducción: el sujeto de la herencia." In *Transmisión de la vida psíquica entre generaciones,* by René Kaës et al. Buenos Aires: Amorrortu.

Kaufman, Susana G. 1998. "Sobre violencia social, trauma y memoria." Paper presented at the Seminar on Collective Memories of Repression. Montevideo: SSRC.

Kolitz, Zvi. 1999. *Yosl Rakover Talks to God.* New York: Pantheon Books.

Koonz, Claudia. 1988. *Mothers in the Fatherland: Women, the Family and Nazi Politics.* New York: St. Martin's Press.

Koonz, Claudia. 1994. "Between Memory and Oblivion: Concentration Camps in German Memory." In *Commemorations: The Politics of National Identity,* edited by John Gillis. Princeton, N.J.: Princeton University Press.

Koselleck, Reinhart. 1985. *Futures Past: On the Semantics of Historical Times.* Cambridge, Mass.: MIT Press.

Kundera, Milan. 1996. *The Book of Laughter and Forgetting.* New York: Harper Perennial.

LaCapra, Dominick. 1998. *History and Memory after Auschwitz.* Ithaca, N.Y.: Cornell University Press.

———. 2001. *Writing History, Writing Trauma.* Baltimore: The Johns Hopkins University Press.

Lanzmann, Claude. 1995. "The Obscenity of Understanding: An Evening with Claude Lanzmann." In *Trauma: Explorations in Memory,* edited by Cathy Caruth. Baltimore: The Johns Hopkins University Press.

Laplanche, Jean, and Jean B. Pontalis. 1981. *Diccionario de psicoanálisis.* Barcelona: Labor.

Laub, Dori. 1992a. "An Event without a Witness: Truth, Testimony and Survival." In *Testimony: Crises of Witnessing in Literature, Psychoanalysis, and History,* by Shoshana Felman and Dori Laub. New York: Routledge.

———. 1992b. "Bearing Witness, or the Vicissitudes of Listening." In *Testimony: Crises of Witnessing in Literature, Psychoanalysis, and History,* by Shoshana Felman and Dori Laub. New York: Routledge.

Lazzara, Michael. 2003. "Tres recorridos de Villa Grimaldi," In *Monumentos, memoriales y marcas territoriales,* by Elizabeth Jelin and Victoria Langland. Madrid and Buenos Aires: Siglo XXI de España Editores/Siglo XXI de Argentina Editores.

Lechner, Norbert. 1999. "Nuestros miedos." In *Chile '98. Entre la II Cumbre y la detención de Pinochet,* FLACSO-Chile. Santiago: FLACSO-Chile.

Lechner, Norbert, and Pedro Güell. 1999. "Construcción social de las memorias en la transición chilena." In *La caja de Pandora: el retorno de la transición chilena,* edited by Amparo Menéndez-Garrión and Alfredo Joignant. Santiago: Planeta.

Levi, Primo. 1988. *The Drowned and the Saved.* New York: Random House.

Leydesdorff, Selma, Luisa Passerini, and Paul Thompson. 1996. Introduction to *Gender and Memory,* edited by Selma Leydesdorff, Luisa Passerini, and Paul Thompson. Oxford: Oxford University Press.

Linenthal, Edward T. 1995. *Preserving Memory: The Struggle to Create America's Holocaust Museum.* New York: Penguin Books.

Loftus, Elizabeth, Mahzarin Banaji, Jonathan Schooler, and Rachael Foster. 1987. "Who Remembers What?: Gender Differences in Memory." *Michigan Quarterly Review* 26.

Loraux, Nicole. 1989. "De la amnistía y su contrario." In *Usos del olvido,* by Yosef Yerushalmi et al. Buenos Aires: Nueva Visión.

Lorenz, Federico. 2002. "¿De quién es el 24 de marzo? Las luchas por la memoria del golpe de 1976." In *Las conmemoraciones: Las disputas en las fechas "in-felices,"* edited by Elizabeth Jelin. Madrid and Buenos Aires: Siglo XXI de España Editores/Siglo XXI de Argentina Editores.

Mannheim, Karl. 1952. *Essays on the Sociology of Knowledge.* New York: Oxford University Press.

Marchesi, Aldo. 2002a. "¿'Guerra' o 'Terrorismo de Estado'? Recuerdos entrentados sobre el pasado reciente uruguayo." In *Las conmemoraciones: Las disputas en las fechas "in-felices,"* edited by Elizabeth Jelin. Madrid and Buenos Aires: Siglo XXI de España Editores/Siglo XXI de Argentina Editores.

———. 2002b. "Las lecciones del pasado. Memoria y ciudadanía en los informes 'nunca mas' del Cono Sur." Unpublished manuscript.

Méndez, Juan E. 1997. "In Defense of Transitional Justice." In *Transitional Justice and the Rule of Law in New Democracies,* edited by James McAdams. Notre Dame, Ind.: University of Notre Dame Press.

Mignone, Emilio F. 1991. *Derechos humanos y sociedad. El caso argentino.* Buenos Aires: Ediciones del Pensamiento Nacional-CELS.

Mostov, Julie. 2000. "Sexing the Nation/Desexing the Body: Politics of National Identity in the Former Yugoslavia." In *Gender Ironies of Nationalism: Sexing the Nation,* edited by Tamar Mayer. London: Routledge.

Namer, Gérard. 1983. *La Commémoration en France, 1944–1982.* Paris: Papyros.

———. 1994. "Postface." In *Les Cadres sociaux de la mémoire,* by Maurice Halbwachs. Paris: Albin Michel.

Nora, Pierre, director. 1984–92. *Les Lieux de mémoire.* 7 vols. Paris: Gallimard.

———. 1996. "Generations." In *Conflicts and Divisions,* vol. 1 of *Realms of Memory: Rethinking the French Past,* under the direction of Pierre Nora. New York: Columbia University Press.

Olavarría, José. 2001. "Hombres e identidades: crisis y globalización." Santiago: FLACSO-Chile, *Documento de Trabajo.*

Olick, Jeffrey K. 1998a. "Memoria colectiva y diferenciación cronológica: historicidad y ámbito público." In *Memoria e historia,* edited by Josefina Cuesta Bustillo. Madrid: Marcial Pons.

———, ed. 1998b. "Special Issue: Memory and the Nation." *Social Science History* 22, 4.

Osiel, Mark. 1997. *Mass Atrocity, Collective Memory and the Law.* New Brunswick, N.J.: Transaction Publishers.

Partnoy, Alicia. 1998. *The Little School: Tales of Disappearance and Survival.* San Francisco: Cleis.

Passerini, Luisa. 1992a. Introduction to *Memory and Totalitarianism,* edited by Luisa Passerini. Oxford: Oxford University Press.

———, ed. 1992b. *Memory and Totalitarianism.* Oxford: Oxford University Press.

———. 1996. "La juventud, metáfora del cambio social (los debates sobre los jóvenes en la Italia fascista y en los Estados Unidos durante los años cincuenta)." In *Historia de los jóvenes. II. La Edad Contemporánea,* under the direction of Giovanni Levi and Jean Claude Schmitt. Madrid: Taurus.

Pollak, Michael. 1989. "Memória, esquecimento, silêncio." *Estudos Históricos* 2, 3.

———. 1990. *L'Expérience concentrationnaire. Essai sur le maintien de l'identité sociale.* Paris: Métailié.

———. 1992. "Memória e identidade social." *Estudos Históricos* 5, 10.

Pollak, Michael, and Nathalie Heinich. 1986. "Le Témoignage." *Actes de la Recherche en Sciences Sociales* 62–63.

Portelli, Alessandro. 1989. "Historia y memoria: la muerte de Luigi Trastulli." *Historia, antropología y fuentes orales* 1.

———. 1997. *The Battle of Valle Giulia: Oral History and the Art of Dialogue.* Madison: University of Wisconsin Press.

————. 1999. *L'Ordine e gia stato eseguito: Roma, le Fosse Aredeatine, la memoria.* Rome: Donzelli.

Punto de vista. 2000. "Arte y política de la memoria. Relatos, símbolos, reconstrucciones, escenas." Special issue, *Punto de Vista 68.*

Renan, Ernest. 2000. "¿Qué es una nación?" In *La invención de la nación,* edited by A. Fernández Bravo. Buenos Aires: Manantial.

Richard, Nelly. 1998. *Residuos y metáforas (Ensayos de crítica cultural sobre el Chile de la Transición).* Santiago: Editorial Cuarto Propio.

————. 2001. "Sitios de la memoria, vaciamiento del recuerdo," *Revista de Crítica Cultural 23.*

Ricoeur, Paul. 1999. *La lectura del tiempo pasado: memoria y olvido,* Madrid: Arrecife-Universidad Autónoma de Madrid.

————. 2000. *La Mémoire, l'histoire, l'oubli.* Paris: Le Seuil.

Rojas, Patricia. 2000. "Los jóvenes y la memoria: una mirada diferente sobre el pasado. Bailando sobre las cenizas." *Puentes* 1, 2.

Rousso, Henry. 1990. *Le Syndrome de Vichy de 1944 à nos jours.* Paris: Gallimard.

————. 2002. *The Haunting Past: History, Memory, and Justice in Contemporary France.* Philadelphia: University of Pennsylvania Press.

Sahlins, Marshall. 1987. *Islands of History.* Chicago: University of Chicago Press.

Salessi, Jorge. 1995. *Médicos maleantes y maricas.* Buenos Aires: Beatriz Viterbo Editora.

Sand, Jordan. 1999. "Historians and Public Memory in Japan: The 'Comfort Women' Controversy. Introduction." *History and Memory: Studies in Representation of the Past* 11, 2.

Schacter, Daniel L. 1996. *Searching for Memory: The Brain, the Mind, and the Past.* New York: Basic Books.

————. 2001. *The Seven Sins of Memory: How the Mind Forgets and Remembers.* Boston: Houghton Mifflin Company.

Scott, James C. 1992. *Hidden Transcripts: Domination and the Arts of Resistance.* New Haven, Conn.: Yale University Press.

Scott, Joan W. 1992. "Experience." In *Feminists Theorize the Political,* edited by Judith Butler and Joan W. Scott. New York: Routledge.

Semprún, Jorge. 1997. *Literature or Life.* New York: Penguin Books.

SERPAJ. 1989. *Uruguay nunca más. Informe sobre la violación al los derechos humanos. 1972–1985.* Montevideo: Servicio Paz y Justicia.

Soares, Gláucio Ary, and Maria Celina D'Araujo, eds. 1994. *21 anos de regime militar: balanços e perspectivas.* Rio de Janeiro: Editora Fundação Getulio Vargas.

Soares, Gláucio Ary, Maria Celina D'Araujo, and Celso Castro, eds. 1995. *A volta aos quartéis: a memória militar sobre a abertura.* Rio de Janeiro: Relume-Demará.

Sommer, Doris. 1991. "Rigoberta's Secrets." *Latin American Perspectives* 70, 18, 3.

Stern, Steve, ed. 1998. *Shining and Other Paths: War and Society in Peru, 1985–1995.* Durham, N.C.: Duke University Press.

Stoll, David. 1999. *Rigoberta Menchú and the Story of All Poor Guatemalans.* Boulder, Colo.: Westview Press.

Sturken, Marita. 1997. *Tangled Memories: The Vietnam War, the AIDS Epidemic, and the Politics of Remembering.* Berkeley: University of California Press.

Tavares, Flávio. 1999. *Memórias do esquecimento.* Sao Paulo: Globo.

Taylor, Diana. 1997. *Disappearing Acts: Spectacles of Gender and Nationalism in Argentina's "Dirty War."* Durham, N.C.: Duke University Press.

Todorov, Tzvetan. 1997. *The Conquest of America: The Question of the Other.* New York: Harper Perennial.

————. 1998. *Les Abus de la mémoire*. Paris: Arléa.

Traverso, Enzo. 2001. "El 'uso público' de la historia." *Puentes* 2, 5.

Valdés, Hernán. 1996. *Tejas verdes. Diario de un campo de concentración en Chile.* Santiago: LOM-CESOC.

Valdés, Teresa. 1999. "Algunas ideas para la consideración de la dimensión de género en la memoria colectiva de la represión." Document prepared for the Social Science Research Council Memory Program.

van Alphen, Ernst. 1997. *Caught by History: Holocaust Effects in Contemporary Art, Literature, and Theory*. Stanford, Calif.: Stanford University Press.

————. 1999. "Symptoms of Discursivity: Experience, Memory, and Trauma." In *Acts of Memory: Cultural Recall in the Present,* edited by Mieke Bal, Jonathan Crewe, and Leo Spitzer. Hanover, N.H.: University Press of New England.

Ventura, Zuenir. 1999. "A nostalgia do não vivido." In *Rebeldes e contestadores. 1968. Brasil, França e Alemanha,* edited by Marco A. García and Maria A. Vieira. Sao Paulo: Fundação Perseu Abramo.

Verbitsky, Horacio. 1995. *El vuelo*. Buenos Aires: Planeta.

Vezzetti, Hugo. 1998. "Activismos de la memoria: el 'escrache.'" *Punto de Vista* 62.

Viezzer, Moema, ed. 1977. *"Si me permiten hablar." Testimonio de Domitila, una mujer de las minas de Bolivia*. Mexico: Siglo XXI.

Wieviorka, Annette. 1998. *L'ère du témoin*. Paris: Plon.

————. 1999. "From Survivor to Witness: Voices from the Shoah." In *War and Remembrance in the Twentieth Century,* edited by Jay Winter and Emmanuel Sivan. Cambridge: Cambridge University Press.

Winter, Jay, and Emmanuel Sivan. 1999. Introduction to *War and Remembrance in the Twentieth Century,* edited by Jay Winter and Emmanuel Sivan. Cambridge: Cambridge University Press.

Yerushalmi, Yosef H. 1996. *Zakhor: Jewish History and Jewish Memory*. Seattle: University of Washington Press.

Yoneyama, Lisa. 1999. *Hiroshima Traces: Time, Space, and the Dialectics of Memory*. Berkeley: University of California Press.

Young, James E. 1993. *The Texture of Memory: Holocaust Memorials and Meaning*. New Haven, Conn.: Yale University Press.

————. 2000. *At Memory's Edge: After-images of the Holocaust in Contemporary Art and Architecture*. New Haven, Conn.: Yale University Press.

Index

Created by Eileen Quam

ELIZABETH JELIN is a professor at the University of Buenos Aires and research director at the Institute of Social and Economic Development (IDES). She is a member of the National Council of Social Research of Argentina and author of numerous articles and essays on human rights and memories of repression in postdictatorial regimes. She is author of *About Women, About Human Rights* and coeditor of *Constructing Democracy: Human Rights, Citizenship, and Society in Latin America.*